SHIRLEY CHISHOLM

SHIRLEY CHISHOLM
THE LAST INTERVIEW
and OTHER CONVERSATIONS

with an introduction by Representative BARBARA LEE

MELVILLE HOUSE
BROOKLYN • LONDON

First Melville House printing: January 2021

Melville House Publishing   Suite 2000
            46 John Street and 16/18 Woodford Road
Brooklyn, NY 11201   London E7 0HA

mhpbooks.com
@melvillehouse

ISBN: 978-1-61219-897-2
ISBN: 978-1-61219-898-9 (eBook)

Printed in the United States of America

1   3   5   7   9   10   8   6   4   2

A catalog record for this book is available from the Library of Congress.

CONTENTS

INTRODUCTION

BARBARA LEE

I would not be Congresswoman Barbara Lee without Congresswoman Shirley Anita Chisholm. Few people have opened more doors for women, children, African Americans and other people of color in elected office than Shirley Chisholm. And without Shirley Chisholm, we would not even think it possible for the first Black woman to serve as vice president of the United States. Nor would we have elected the first African American man as the first president of the United States.

I first recognized her impact when I attended Mills College in Oakland, California. I was a young, single mom on public assistance and food stamps at the time. I was serving as president of the Black Student Union, volunteering with the Black Panther Party, and raising two young boys. My professor in our government class assigned us fieldwork on a presidential campaign. George McGovern, Hubert Humphrey, and Ed Muskie were the candidates, but my mind was already made up. I was going to flunk this assignment. I had never flunked a class in my life, but those men didn't represent the issues important to me as a Black single mother—issues like childcare, public education, universal health care, and ending poverty.

And then I met Shirley Chisholm. I invited Congresswoman Chisholm to Mills to address the Black Student Union as the first African American woman elected to Congress. Of course, I had no idea until she said it during her speech that SHE was in fact running for president. I couldn't believe it. Now THIS was a candidate I could believe in. She was a champion of children and struggling families. She spoke fluent Spanish and fought for the rights of immigrants. She stood up against racism and sexism. She opposed the war in Vietnam. She was doing what she knew to be right—regardless of the criticism. She was bold, she was courageous—she was "unbought and unbossed." As soon as she finished her speech, I rushed to her, told her about my assignment and my reluctance to get involved in politics because neither party offered an agenda I could support.

She told me that she needed help organizing in California. But when she asked me if I was registered to vote, I admitted that I was not. She was not pleased. She looked at me, with a look I will never forget, and said: "Little girl, you can't change the system if you on the outside looking in. Register to vote." So, I registered to vote, organized the Northern California campaign from my class at Mills College, got an A, and went to the convention in Miami as a Shirley Chisholm delegate. The rest is history. She became my mentor, inspiration, and confidant when I began my public service career as an intern and then a senior staff member in the office of our beloved, the late Congressman Ron Dellums.

On a personal note, Mrs. C, as some called her, loved to dance and have fun. She attended my late mother's 70th birthday party. They both were the last ones on the dance floor at 2 a.m.

Shirley valued her privacy and told me to cherish what little private life you have even as a public person. I will always remember going on vacation in the Virgin Islands determined to find Congresswoman Chisholm's house on St. Thomas. Luckily, a taxi driver took me there and she was shocked to see me. She was relaxing in her pool, but she was so kind and greeted me with open arms, even took pictures with me. As I reflect on that day, knowing how she valued her private moments, this act of generosity toward a young, adoring student was an example of her kindness and understanding of the importance of her relationship to me as a role model and mentor.

Shirley Chisholm was a leader in its purest form. She got people off the sidelines and involved in the process. When I reflect on the impact she had on me, others before me, and the impact she'll certainly have on those after me, I can't help but be reminded of one of her famous quotes: "You don't make progress by standing on the sidelines, whimpering and complaining. You make progress by implementing ideas."

She knew that her ideas would only be implemented if we brought more people into the discussion. More women, more people of color, more young people. And when I look at Congress now, her vision is being realized. There are 105 women now serving in Congress, and Black women are continuing to lead. We now have more than 20 Black women serving in Congress. That's because of her.

This collection of her interviews, from her first major profile to her last interview, indicates that her focus never shifted. She remained steadfast in her fight for the people she represented. Her day-to-day life operating in our legislative body was laden with sexism, racism, and bigotry, and her career and legacy serve as a lesson in true resiliency.

Let's be clear: Congresswoman Chisholm's legacy goes far beyond her impact within history books. She was more than the first Black woman elected to Congress. She was more than the first Black woman to run for president of the United States. She should also be remembered for what she accomplished during her tenure in Congress. She used her office to fight for low-income families, hungry school kids, single moms, and immigrants. She was instrumental in creating the national school lunch program, expanding the food stamp program, and establishing the Special Supplemental Nutrition Program for Women, Infants and Children, commonly known as WIC. She made this country a better place.

Today, nearly fifty years after Congresswoman Shirley Chisholm first mounted her historic run for president as the first Black woman to do so, a Black woman was selected as the vice president on a major party ticket. My career in public service, and the careers of countless other women of color, can be attributed to trailblazers like Shirley Chisholm. Congresswoman Chisholm showed me the power of "unbought and unbossed" women of color to change our country. Her words guide my work in Congress every day, and her vision for America is one that we all should continue striving for, with the hope it will soon be realized.

SHIRLEY CHISHOLM

THIS IS FIGHTING SHIRLEY CHISHOLM

INTERVIEW BY SUSAN BROWNMILLER
THE NEW YORK TIMES
APRIL 13, 1969

The annual founders'-day luncheon of the Delta Sigma Theta sorority was held this January at the Americana Hotel. The occasion represented a triple honor for the Brooklyn alumnae chapter of Delta, one of three ranking and fiercely competitive Negro sororities in the country. It was Brooklyn's turn to play hostess to the national; the guest speaker was the Honorable Shirley Chisholm, first black Congresswoman in America; and, coup of coups, in the secret ceremony before the luncheon the chapter was privileged to initiate into Delta the lady of the hour herself.

"Soror" Chisholm cut an imposing figure on the dais. Small, dark, ramrod straight, she was outfitted in a blue-and-gilt brocade suit with matching turban. Her black-rimmed eyeglasses were firmly planted above her wide nose. Her bearing gave her the look of a visiting queen rather than Delta's newest initiate. When it was her turn to speak, Mrs. Chisholm arose with her prepared text.

She has a quality that is rare in any woman—the ability to speak forcefully before an audience. On this particular afternoon, the former schoolteacher began by enunciating each syllable with biting clarity, her West Indian accent rising and falling in controlled cadence, her strongly sibilant "s" forming a pleasant rhythmic counterpoint to the clipped words. Midway through her effort (an inspirational plea for higher horizons), Mrs. Chisholm smiled broadly. As she put aside her notes, her voice lost some of its didactic schoolmarm flavor and took on an earthier cadence of the streets.

"You have *no idea* what those people in Washington with their hands on the power have been plotting and planning for us. Let me tell you. Do not be complacent. The Man says *he knows* we ain't never gonna come together." The audience rumbled its understanding of her warning. Surveying the ballroom from left to right, Mrs. Chisholm went on. "Oh, everyone is being *so kind* to me. They have *such* good advice. They tell me, Shirley, you're just a freshman and you have to keep quiet as a freshman—." She paused for effect as some of the women giggled.

"I listen sweetly to them and then I say, 'Gentlemen, thank you for your advice. I understand what you're saying. But when I get up there on the floor of Congress, I'm sure you'll understand that I am speaking with the pent-up emotions of the community.'" She grinned. "One thing the people in Washington and New York are afraid of in Shirley Chilsholm is HER MOUTH." The audience roared.

A few days later, Representative Chisholm returned to Washington and began her fight to change her assignment from a House Agriculture subcommittee on Forestry and Rural Villages to something more relevant to her Bedford-Stuyvesant community. (Mrs. Chisholm had hoped for Education and Labor.) She approached Speaker John McCormack, who told her, she reports, to accept the assignment and "be a good soldier." She brooded about that for a while, she says, and then decided, "That's why the country is the way it is." Mrs. Chisholm then placed an amendment before the House Democratic caucus to remove her name from the Agriculture Committee, aware that she was taking an unprecedented step—bucking the powerful Wilbur Mills of Arkansas, chairman of the House Ways and Means Committee and the man who parcels out committee assignments to his fellow Democrats. According to Mrs. Chisholm, Mills tried to call her bluff in caucus. "Will the gentlewoman from Brooklyn withdraw her amendment?" he intoned. Mrs. Chisholm says she was particularly tickled by "gentlewoman," but otherwise remained unmoved. Mrs. Chisholm was removed from Agriculture and later assigned to Veterans' Affairs. The Chisholm balk remains the most vivid sign of life in the Ninety-First Congress.

Shirley Chisholm is true grit. Her comet-like rise from clubhouse worker to Representative in the United States Congress was no accident of the political heavens. It was accomplished by the wiles of a steely politician with a belief in her own abilities which at times approaches an almost Messianic fervor. "My rise has been constantly fighting," she likes to say. "And I have had to fight doubly hard because I am a woman. I am a very different sort of person than usually emerges on the political scene." It's an accurate self-assessment. "The nation's first black Congresswoman"—or "first black woman Congressman," as she prefers to put it—does not begin to explain who Shirley Chisholm is. But "the first black," etc., is not how she wishes to be remembered. "I'd like them to say that Shirley Chisholm had *guts*. That's how I'd like to be remembered."

There is a saying about women who hold elective office—that most of them got there on a "widow's mandate." It certainly holds true for Edna Kelly, the Congressional veteran who was unceremoniously bumped from her seat last year when Brooklyn's Twelfth Congressional District was redrawn to carve out a largely black constituency. Mrs. Kelly was brought into politics by Irwin Steingut, then the minority leader of the State Assembly, when her husband, a judge, was killed in an automobile crash. Her nineteen-year record in Congress was, at best, mediocre. Early in 1968, the State Legislature, under Federal Court order to correct population inequities in some Congressional districts, revamped the lines in central Brooklyn in such a manner that Mrs. Kelly was wiped off the political map. Mrs. Kelly, until that time a loyal soldier in the Brooklyn Democratic organization, cried "betrayal." She charged that county leader Stanley Steingut, the son of her first patron, had willfully forced her political extinction. She eventually delivered her own coup de grâce by running a hopeless primary race in a neighboring district against Emanuel Celler.

The new Twelfth Congressional District was anchored to the heavily black Bedford-Stuyvesant neighborhood (Mrs. Chisholm's home territory), with slices of Crown Heights, Bushwick and Williamsburg around the edges. The new district was about 80 percent Democratic. Its ethnic breakdown was 70 percent black and 30 percent white. There were Puerto Ricans in Williamsburg (Mrs. Chisholm speaks

Spanish fluently), Italians in the Bushwick section, and Jews in Crown Heights. Mrs. Chisholm's survey of the election rolls ("Before I make a move, I analyze everything," she says, eyes snapping) turned up one additional demographic factor which possibly eluded other Congressional hopefuls. The Twelfth had ten thousand to thirteen thousand more registered women voters than men. Before the ink was dry on the new district's lines, Shirley Chisholm put in her bid.

While Bedford-Stuyvesant was the heart of the new Twelfth Congressional District, the Unity Democratic Club, the regular Democratic organization for the Fifty-Fifth State Assembly District, was the strongest political club in Bedford-Stuyvesant. Unity was founded in 1960 around the person of Thomas R. Jones, a politically active lawyer, and the club won its spurs in 1962 with the election of Jones to State Assembly and to the district leadership, beating out Sam Berman's old-line Jewish organization in the changing neighborhood. Tom Jones was Unity's standard-bearer and guiding light, but when he was offered a civil court judgeship in 1964, he accepted—and removed himself from the local political fray. It was at this point that Shirley Chisholm announced she would seek Jones's assembly seat.

"They were shocked," Mrs. Chisholm remembers. "It was the first time a black woman had sought elective office in Brooklyn. But I knew I could do it. I felt strong enough. There were people in that clubhouse who were saying, 'Why not give Chisholm a chance? She's *got it*. She can *lead*.' So I told the club's executive committee, 'If you need to have a discussion, have a discussion. But it makes no difference to me. I intend to fight.'" Other who were members of the executive committee at the time remember it differently. Particularly, they recall a stormy session with tears when it looked for a moment as if Jones might stay in the Assembly after all. In any event, Mrs. Chisholm got the Unity Club's endorsement and went on to win the 1964 primary and the general election. Because of the reapportionment, she had to run again in 1965 and '66. "I proved to be the top vote-getter," she says grimly. "I always pulled higher than the top of the ticket."

In Albany, Mrs. Chisholm also proved an able enough legislator. Her name was attached to the Assembly side of the first legislation extending unemployment insurance benefits to domestic workers, and she plumped hard in committee and on the Assembly floor for the SEEK program, a higher-education plan that enables worthy disadvantaged students who make low-aptitude scores to enter universities and receive intensive remedial aid. Assemblyman Albert H. Blumenthal, the newly appointed "deputy" minority leader, recalls Mrs. Chisholm as "a very tough lady, likable, but a loner. Unlike other women in the Legislature, she was never afraid to jump into a debate. Shirley was never hysterical, she never flailed. She knew what she wanted to say and she said it well. She wasn't quick to make up her mind, but when she did, you couldn't blast her out of it. Enemies like Shirley," Blumenthal adds half-humorously, "nobody needs in politics." (For those who like to keep their records straight, Mrs. Chisholm was the *second* Black woman to sit in the Assembly. The first was Bessie Buchanan, the coquettish wife of a Harlem businessman, whose major legislative effort over the years was devoted to getting a certain song officially declared the New York State anthem.)

Albany is a dreary place for legislators once the day's session is over, and most of "the boys" make the best of it by breaking up into congenial groups at night to make the rounds of restaurants, movies and bars. "My impression of Shirley," Blumenthal says, "is that she preferred to take her work back to the hotel with her at night." Blumenthal is not an insensitive fellow. He admitted he couldn't recall anyone in his crowd ever *extending* a dinner invitation to the legislator from Brooklyn, but he didn't know precisely why.

"I don't blame the fellows for not asking me out to dinner," Mrs. Chisholm says reflectively. "I think there was a little fear of 'How do we handle her socially?' Men don't like independent women. Not many knew I was a regular gal. I think they were afraid to take the chance. I ate most of the time in my room. I had the TV and I read and I did my legislative homework. I went to bed early." Stiffening, she concludes, "I do not care for the night life of the New York State Legislature."

One thing that was noticeable about Assemblywoman Chisholm was that her relations with Brooklyn leader Stanley Steingut appeared to be considerably strained. Blumenthal believes it all began over what Chisholm concluded was a personal slight she had once received from the brusque former county chairman. The inscrutable, tight-lipped Steingut professes to be "honestly baffled" by Chisholm's actions. Chisholm says, "Those that know Stanley and those that know me know the story." At any rate, many of Chisholm's votes, both in the Assembly and in Democratic party councils, were not designed to make Mrs. Steingut happy. Even as recently as this past fall, when she was out of the Assembly, she let it be known that she personally preferred Moe Weinstein of Queens to Steingut for the Assembly's minority leadership.

Stanley Steingut is not the only man who professes to be baffled by Chisholm. Her relations with black politicians in Brooklyn have often been bumpy. One man who is an expert on Shirley Chisholm—her husband, Conrad—offers this explanation: "Mrs. Chisholm competes very well with everybody."

Conrad Chisholm is a pipe-smoking, outwardly affable, solidly built man who is unquestionably devoted to his wife's career. The two are very close (their nineteen-year marriage has been childless) and it amuses Mrs. Chisholm that those who don't know her husband are quick to pigeonhole him. "They always assume that my husband must be a tiny little shrimp of a weakling," she says with a grin.

Mr. Chisholm is also amused by outsiders' assumptions about his marriage. "I am not threatened by her in any way," he says firmly. "I grew up secure. I'm West Indian. Early in our marriage I saw Shirley's ability to get things done. I decided she'd be the star in our family, she'd get the billing. I push her in any way I can." Chisholm is a former private investigator who specialized in knocking holes in compensation claims against the railroads, and when the mood strikes him, he can spin intricate tales of the ruses he employed to trap less than honest claimants. He is now a senior investigator with New York City's Department of Social Service, in charge of evaluating Medicaid applications. Taking a passing interest in politics himself, he has been an election district captain in the Unity Club.

Although Mrs. Chisholm was the first in her district to announce for Congress in 1968, she didn't have the field to herself for very long. Judge Tom Jones—who had opted for the bench four years before—indicated that he was interested. Conrad Chisholm says that well before the petition period began, a "Jones for Congress" storefront "sprang up" on Fulton Street, although Jones disclaimed he had encouraged it. Thomas R. Fortune, the man who replaced Jones as Unity Club leader (and the man who this year replaced Mrs. Chisholm in Albany), gets a funny look on his face when Jones's Congressional interest in mentioned. "He came around to the club," Fortune admits, "but there wasn't much support for him. You know, a judge is supposed to be above politics, and Jones hadn't been to the club much in the last few years."

Jones was known as Senator Robert F. Kennedy's man in Bedford-Stuyvesant. Kennedy had put his prestige behind a Bedford-Stuyvesant redevelopment project, and he had named Jones to direct the "community" end of the program. Jones was the man that Kennedy talked to in Bedford-Stuyvesant; Kennedy did not take any notice of Shirley Chisholm. "Kennedy didn't understand the district," Mrs. Chisholm says, her eyes narrowing. "I was the top vote-getter, but Kennedy never sought me out." Her eyes narrow more as she adds, "I think there were some people who kept him from me."

Mrs. Chisholm was convinced that Jones had won support from Robert Kennedy for his Congressional bid. Jones is convincing when he admits—with considerable chagrin—the he went to Kennedy for his help, but that Kennedy told him he would be "more valuable" as head of the Bedford-Stuyvesant

Restoration Corporation. Jones eventually declined to make the race; he accepted instead a nomination for a State Supreme Court judgeship.

State Senator William C. Thompson, who had also declared early, was somewhat ambivalent at first, according to the Chisholms. Right up to the deadline for filing nominating petitions, they say, Thompson had assured Shirley that he wasn't going to run. They point to his final decision to make the race as proof that he had a tacit understanding with Robert Kennedy—*and* Stanley Steingut—two men who had considerable clout with the white district leaders whose domains lay partially within the borders of the Twelfth Congressional District. "Willie felt the white boys were going to get out the vote for him," Mrs. Chisholm says flatly.

The third candidate who ran in the Democratic primary was Dolly Robinson, a former co-leader of Bertram Baker's. Assemblyman Baker of the Fifty-Sixth A.D. (and the co-sponsor of the famous Metcalf-Baker open-housing law) had his own axes to grind in the primary. Thompson and he had had a serious falling out over a past judicial contest, and Thompson had formed his own club in Baker's district and was now challenging the aging Baker for the leadership. Baker toyed briefly with the idea of supporting Judge Jones—but Jones was a Kennedy man and Baker was strong for Johnson and Humphrey. Baker felt he couldn't quite support Mrs. Chisholm, either. On the floor of the Assembly one day, Mrs. Chisholm had made an unfortunate and devastating wisecrack concerning Baker. His pride wounded on all fronts, Baker put up a spoiler candidate. "But I think he was glad I won," Mrs. Chisholm relates. "He came over and hugged me afterward."

With Dolly Robinson running as the Humphrey candidate, and Thompson looking like the Kennedy candidate, who was there left for Mrs. Chisholm? The Coalition for a Democratic Alternative began getting little nibbles from her. The nibbles culminated in a half-hour telephone conversation between candidate Chisholm and candidate Eugene McCarthy. (The call was placed by the Senator.) Mrs. Chisholm discontinued her tenuous relations with the McCarthy people after Robert Kennedy died.

It was sticky politics, this three-way race for a black Democratic nominee, and it was for this reason, says Stanley Steingut, that he chose to remain aloof from it. "Why should I get involved in a battle between Brooklyn legislators?" he asks. Mrs. Chisholm, however, remains firm in her conviction that Steingut *did* get involved, and in Thompson's corner. "Never before in the history of Kings County did a county leader throw the choice of Congressman to the people," she exclaims. That is probably true, and Mrs. Chisholm made capital of it in her campaign. Her slogan, "Unbought and Unbossed," managed to tar Thompson with the support he might or might *not* have had.

Mrs. Chisholm likes to campaign. "I am the people's politician," she says. "If the day should ever come when the people can't save me, I'll know I'm finished. That's when I'll go back to being a professional educator." The candidate chose as her campaign manager an old pro named Wesley Holder who had been in and out of various Bedford-Stuyvesant political factions for more than a decade. She enlisted Julius C. C. Edelstein, a former factotum in reform politics and a

onetime Wagner aide, as financial adviser and behind-the-
scenes *éminence grise*. In addition to the forces of the Unity
Club, her home base, Mrs. Chisholm developed a small army
of women who roamed the district in her behalf.

"The women are fierce about Shirley," says her husband.
"She can pick up the phone and call two hundred women and
they'll be here in an hour. And she gives them nothing more
than a 'thank you' and a buffet supper."

"It stings the professional boys," adds the Congresswoman. "All I have to say is, 'We gotta go to war.'"

Chisholm's war was fought from a sound truck. The way
she recounts it, the truck would pull up to a housing project
such as the Brevoort Houses with a retinue of private cars in
its wake: "I'd get up there and say *Ladies and Gentlemen of
the Brevoort Houses, this is Fighting Shirley Chisholm coming
through.* I have a way of talking that does something to the
people," she adds. "Meanwhile, my workers would scatter in
all directions with shopping bags filled with literature. We'd
hand out two thousand pieces at each stop. I have a theory
about campaigning. You have to let them *feel* you."

Despite the knockdown, drag-out contest, the voter
turnout on June 18 in the Twelfth District was among the
lowest in the city. Pundits had predicted a Thompson victory.
"You could have won any kind of money on that," Tommy
Fortune chuckles. But when the figures were in, the Unity
Club had given Chisholm a 1,265-vote cushion. It was more
than enough to cover her losses in other areas. Chisholm won
her primary by 788 votes.

In July, the victorious nominee entered the hospital for
an operation on a massive fibroid tumor. At the Democratic
convention in Chicago (which she sat out in a hotel room),

Mrs. Chisholm emerged as the choice of all factions of New York State's delegation for the post of national committee-woman, replacing Edna Kelly.

Anyone with less than a keen interest in local politics might have concluded that "what was happening" in Bedford-Stuyvesant was the campaign of James Farmer. The former national director of CORE had been at loose ends since he resigned his post a few years back to head up a Johnson Administration literacy program which never came into being. Early in the spring, Farmer announced his entry into the Twelfth District race as the candidate of the Liberal party. In May, the nationally known civil rights spokesman was accorded the Republican designation.

Farmer's Republican blessing did not come easily. According to Mrs. Chisholm, who maintains that three of the local Republican leaders worked quietly for her in the general election, the Brooklyn Republicans were subjected to outside pressure from as far away as Senator Charles Percy of Illinois. "They felt it was a terrible intrusion," she states. "It was saying to them, 'You don't have anybody worthwhile for this $30,000 [now $42,500] fruitcake.' It was a slap in the community's face. Everybody, Republican, Democrat, black and white, male and female, resented the intrusion."

Farmer, who lived in Manhattan took an apartment on Herkimer Street near Nostrand Avenue in the district for a mailing address. He attempted *rapprochement* with Sonny Carson's breakaway chapter of Brooklyn CORE, which had been making anti-Farmer noises in the community and had even tried to field a Congressional candidate of its own. Brooklyn CORE was an embarrassment to the former CORE

chief, but the eventual détente did little to help him. Sonny
Carson's strength, whatever it might be, was not on the election rolls. Nixon-Agnew at the head of the Republican ticket
also proved embarrassing. Farmer favored Humphrey (and so
did the Liberal party—strongly). His strategy was to attack
the Nixon-Agnew team freely during the campaign and urge
the electorate to go into the polls and "Vote Farmer First."

Bongo drums on the streets—a regular part of Farmer's campaign in Bedford-Stuyvesant—projected an image
redolent of Africa and manhood. Farmer's handbills stressed
the need for "a man's voice" in Washington. This may have
been what the Moynihan Report was talking about, but it
didn't sit well with Shirley Chisholm. In her Washington office desk Mrs. Chisholm keeps a long scathing poem called
"Mrs. Moynihan in Bedford-Stuyvesant" written by a (male)
student in Harvard's Afro-American Association. "Of course
we have to help black men," the Congresswoman says. "But
not at the expense of our own personalities as women. The
black man must step forward, but that does not mean *we* have
to step back. Where have we ever been? For the last fifteen
years, black men have held political office, not women."

The black male *mystique* stung Shirley Chisholm (she recalls
walking into public meetings and being greeted by the catcall,
"Here comes the black matriarch!"), but the unspoken truth
of the Farmer campaign was that Farmer's "black male" image
had a double edge. The women of Bedford-Stuyvesant knew
without being reminded that James Farmer had a white wife.

The Farmer-vs-Chisholm campaign attracted national coverage, but from network television down to *The*

Village Voice, the focus was on James Farmer and not Shirley Chisholm. The Chisholm camp found N.B.C.'s weekend special, "The Campaign and the Candidates," particularly galling. The half-hour show devoted itself almost exclusively to Farmer. N.B.C. newsfolk still insist that they were justified. Farmer was a "national figure" who made the story "newsworthy." His campaign was "highly visible and colorful" while Mrs. Chisholm's was restricted because she was still recuperating from her operation. But from Chisholm's vantage point, and the vantage point of hindsight, the show was a serious misreading of local politics.

One N.B.C. reporter, the local station's Gabe Pressman, did not believe that Farmer was a shoo-in. Pressman spent a half day on the Chisholm campaign trail and returned to his office convinced that Mrs. Chisholm had it. He had accompanied her to a project, the Alabama Houses, and the response she had received there was convincing stuff. Pressman was right, of course, but he never knew how carefully his day with Mrs. Chisholm had been planned. The Unity Club's captain for the Alabama Houses was none other than Conrad Chisholm.

When Mrs. Chisholm is feeling sour, she says that "any Republican the local leaders might have chosen would have run better than Farmer." When she is feeling more charitable, she avows that, "Farmer ran about as well as any Republican could" in the district. There is no doubt that Farmer picked up a number of "identification votes" from those who went into the polls and pulled the lever for the name they most readily recognized. And, according to Julius Edelstein, "The male thing made inroads among

voters who sincerely, if mistakenly, chose to believe in it."
But Farmer's entry into the race had been a mistake from
the very beginning. Mrs. Chisholm whipped "the national
figure" (her pet name for him) by almost 2½ to 1. (Getting whipped by a woman did no permanent damage to
either James Farmer or William C. Thompson, apparently.
Thompson was subsequently named to fill a City Council
vacancy; President Nixon appointed Farmer Assistant Secretary of Health, Education and Welfare.)

Washington's introduction to Fighting Shirley Chisholm
and Representative Chisholm's introduction to Washington were not accomplished without a few surprises on both
sides. A couple of weeks after Mrs. Chisholm moved into a
furnished apartment in one of the capital's newer residen-
tial complexes, the apartment was broken into while she was
weekending in New York. The thief or thieves made off with
her new Washington wardrobe, a collection of knit suits.
Mrs. Chisholm moved to another address and charged that
the theft had all the markings of an "inside job."

Mrs. Chisholm would just as soon not have talked to
anyone (except the police) about the burglary, but she finds
it difficult to escape the attentions of the news media. It is a
rare day when her appointments calendar does not show at
least one interview—she is good copy for political reporters
across the United States, for European journalists, members
of the Negro press, the women's pages, the college press, and
Washington's regular Capitol Hill corps, and all of the above-
named's radio and TV counterparts. In fact, anyone with a
notebook or a tape recorder considers Mrs. Chisholm fair
game.

Sheer instinct for self-survival has led her to develop a set patter, with variations as the mood or occasion strikes her. Chisholm on Chisholm does not always achieve its intended effect. A speech she gave at a gala press reception went something like this, according to the notes of one women's page reporter: "They call me Fighting Shirley Chisholm. My mother tells me I was born fighting. She says I was kicking so hard in the womb, she knew I was aching to get out and fight." According to the reporter, the raised eyebrows around the room were something to see. "My dear!" the reporter says. "The womb? Really. Maurine Neuberger didn't open her mouth the first year she was here." The womb image may have been a bit much even for Chisholm, and she dropped it after that night.

Shirley St. Hill Chisholm was born forty-four years ago in Brooklyn, shipped back to Barbados at age three to live with her grandmother, and returned to Brooklyn at age eleven. Her father was an unskilled laborer and her mother worked as a domestic to help support her brood. Shirley was the oldest of four girls. A more credible anecdote of her early precocity she recounts with pride: "Mother always said that even when I was three, I used to get the six- and seven-year-old kids on the block and punch them and say, 'Listen to me.' I was a fat little thing then, believe it or not."

Little Shirley grew up with a strong sense of her own destiny. Her early heroes were Mary McLeod Bethune, Harriet Tubman and Susan B. Anthony. Miss Anthony, the homeliest of the suffragettes, was one of the movement's best speakers. In her Brooklyn campaign, Mrs. Chisholm would reel off a long quotation from Miss Anthony ("The hour is come when the women will no longer be the passive recipients. . .") when she was bothered by male hecklers on street corners. "It always stopped them cold," she reports.

Mrs. Chisholm matriculated at Brooklyn College (she won a scholarship and was in the debating society) and took her master's at Columbia. She went the route that bright black women who are determined to better their lives find most readily open to them: she became a teacher, and served for a time as director of a day-care center. She was introduced to her future husband in Brooklyn. Conrad was from Jamaica. "I used to kid him," she says, "that Jamaican men always want the best so he just *had* to marry a Barbadian girl." The Chisholms have made a ritual of taking their yearly vacation in the islands. (This summer the routine may be broken. Mrs. Chisholm has her eye on an African tour.)

When Mrs. Chisholm began to fashion her political career, her husband assigned himself the task of shepherding her from meeting to meeting, trying to get her to appointments within a reasonable time (Mrs. Chisholm always runs late). In Washington, Mrs. Chisholm is escorted to and from her engagements off the Hill by any one of her office assistants. Representative Chisholm's office, on the street floor of the Longworth Building, has a staff of six women, four black and two white, with a median age of twenty-four. Three of the girls were aides to former Congressman Joseph Resnick of Ellenville. The Chisholm outer office has an unusual feminine ambience: the girls are more attuned to each other's incipient moods and sniffles than a male or mixed staff would be. None of the girls are from Brooklyn. Mrs. Chisholm was forced to sacrifice some patronage for a staff which knew its way around the Hill. (Maneuvering the marble corridors of Congress is a challenge to any freshman legislator.)

Apart from an abrasive administrative assistant, who is working her way into the job (she held a lesser post with Resnick), and whom Mrs. Chisholm defends vociferously ("She's tough," says the Congresswoman, "and that's what I need."), the staff appears to be hardworking and courteous. "But you can tell Mrs. Chisholm's new," sighed one of the girls on a recent morning. "She still wants us to let her open all the mail that's marked personal." (Mail to the Chisholm office in these early weeks, admittedly a staggering load, has had a tendency to go unanswered.)

On any given day, the Chisholm office is bolstered by no fewer than three student volunteers who are there to "observe" for their college courses and to "pitch in" wherever they can be of use, which generally means running to the library to research facts for legislative aide Shirley Downs. Miss Downs, along with secretary Carolyn Jones, has managed to bring whatever order there is to the hectic office. She marvels over her new boss: "She's like a vacuum cleaner. I mark stuff for her to read and the next day she comes in and says, 'Let's get together at two o'clock and discuss it.' She reads anything and everything. The other day she waltzed out of here with 'The Valachi Papers.'"

Mrs. Chisholm is valiantly trying to arrange her Washington life along the pattern of her stay in Albany. Beset by telephone calls, both political and social, from Washington's Negro community, which feels that the nation's first black Congresswoman would make an important addition to their parties and their causes, Mrs. Chisholm has tried to make her Washington apartment into something of a retreat, and she guards her after-hours privacy like a watchdog, preferring solitude to sociability. Her home telephone number in Washington is a closely kept secret, and she recently disconnected her listed New York telephone number and arranged to have the calls transferred to her newly opened district office on Eastern Parkway, manned by former campaign manager Wesley Holder. (Mrs. Chisholm is available to her constituents at her Eastern Parkway office on Fridays from 5:00 to 8:00 p.m.)

The November elections brought the number of Negro representatives in the House up to nine, "hardly an explosion of black political power," as *Ebony* magazine put it, but a tangible gain. Joining Mrs. Chisholm as freshman Democrats are the gregarious Louis Stokes of Ohio, that state's first black representative, and smooth, young William L. Clay of Missouri, a first for his state as well. With Powell back (though just barely) and John Conyers of Michigan facing stiff competition from the newcomers (Conyers moved into a power vacuum during the Powell difficulties), there is active speculation on the Hill over the eventual pecking order of the new black lineup. "We watch each other," Mrs. Chisholm admits, "and the boys keep a special eye on Conyers." (The "watching" is done informally. No "black caucus" has yet emerged in the Ninety-First Congress.)

According to some experienced Washington hands, Mrs. Chisholm's well-publicized battle over her committee assignment ended in a standoff. Mrs. Chisholm is inclined to disagree. She did manage to turn an unexpected spotlight on the House's seniority system, and, she is quick to point out, the Veterans Affairs Committee *does* have some relevance to her community. There is a Veterans Administration hospital in Brooklyn and Mrs. Chisholm intends to use her position on the committee to "make people more aware of their eligibility for the hospital and other veterans' benefits."

Apart from the committee-assignment squabble, Mrs. Chisholm's legislative activities in the first sluggish weeks of Congress have included endorsing a fistful of bills sponsored by other black and/or liberal Congressmen, and making a fiery maiden speech. She has lent her name to an omnibus $30-billion-per-annum "Full Opportunity Act" put forward by Conyers; a Martin Luther King national holiday bill, also introduced by Conyers; a bill to set up a study commission on Afro-American history and culture, sponsored by James Scheuer of New York; a bill to abolish the House Un-American Activities Committee (dropped into the legislative hopper by Don Edwards of California before HUAC underwent its name change to the House Internal Security Committee); a bill to broaden the powers of the Department of Housing and Urban Development, sponsored by Jonathan Bingham of New York; a bill to create a Cabinet-level Department of Consumer Affairs, sponsored by Benjamin Rosenthal of New York; a bill to repeal provisions of the Social Security Act which limit the number of children in a family that can receive welfare payments under the Aid to Dependent Children clauses (sponsored by James Corman of California); and a resolution urging that food and medical supplies be rushed to the Biafra-Nigeria war zone. Mrs. Chisholm expects to work up legislation of her own on man-power training, and would like to initiate a federal program along the lines of New York State's SEEK.

In her maiden speech late last month, Mrs. Chisholm (who came late to an anti-Vietnam war position) declared that she would oppose every defense money bill "until the time comes when our values and priorities have been turned right side up again" and called upon "every mother, wife and widow in this land" to support her position. Whether the fiercely idealistic, unbargaining Chisholm manner is as effective in Washington as in Brooklyn remains to be seen. (Also during her first weeks in Congress, Chisholm let it be known that she had quite a flair for keeping her name before the public: she announced she was "seriously considering" becoming a candidate for Mayor of New York.)

Like most other Congressmen from New York, Mrs. Chisholm commutes, arriving in Brooklyn on Thursday evening and taking the last Sunday shuttle back to Washington. After her victory, the Chisholms gave up their rented quarters and bought their first home, a nine-room attached row house on St. John's Place in the district. A large, hand-colored photograph of Mrs. Chisholm dominates one wall of the new living room, the décor of which is decidedly Victorian. A baby grand piano is squeezed into a space along the opposite wall. Next to reading, the Congresswoman prefers to relax by playing the piano. Mrs. Chisholm could never be called an underachiever. She also likes to dance, and has entered and won several Latin dance competitions. And she is a bit of a writer; some of her poems, mainly political, have appeared in the Albany papers and *The Amsterdam News.*

The new Chisholm residence is just outside the Unity Club's territory, and while this happenstance in itself is not particularly significant, Mrs. Chisholm made it plain after her election that she intends to be the Congressman for the whole district—a statement interpreted by some observers to mean that she intends to cut her ties with Unity. Her future relations with Unity are one subject which the outspoken lady refuses to clarify. Tommy Fortune says merely, "She knows better than to pick a battle with her own leader and her home base." Fortune, who admits that he sometimes finds it easier to deal with Congressman Chisholm through Conrad Chisholm, is one who did *not* think Chisholm's balk on the Agriculture assignment was good politics.

Mrs. Chisholm does not care to be beholden to anybody. "Don't talk to me about those reform Coalition for a Democratic Alternative people," she explodes. "They always try to claim me for their own because my views on legislation are progressive. Reformers? I have another name for them. We in the black community have to be very careful whom we associate with. My husband is a former private investigator. I have dossiers on people." Whether or not she actually has dossiers is debatable. (Unity Club members remember hints about dossiers in the old days.) Mrs. Chisholm's sharp tongue is hardly reserved for reformers. She doesn't mind referring to super-black militants as "woolly-heads" and "spear carriers" when it is *they* who get her back up, as they did at one memorable meeting of the Bedford-Stuyvesant Restoration Corporation. White liberals? Mrs. Chisholm says archly, "Don't you know that white liberals are our favorite parlor conversation?" The result of Mrs. Chisholm's free-swinging rhetoric is to keep her allies and potential allies slightly off-balance, which is no doubt where she wants them. "Some of these politicians," she concedes, "think I'm half crazy, that I don't know what I'm doing. Good. Let them think that," she finishes coolly.

She is expert at picking her way through the thorny racial issues facing black and white these days and she exhibits a fine disregard for both the fears and the panaceas now in vogue. Black anti-Semitism is one issue for which she has little patience. "I wish to God the mass media would stop playing it up," she implores. "Don't they understand that what is going on is an *anti-establishment* feeling? Of course it is the Jewish landlord and the Jewish shopkeeper in the ghetto that the black man sees and reacts against, but it is not anti-Semitism that is at work. What worries me more is this new restraint I see on the part of white liberals who profess not to understand why blacks are rising up in such hostile fashion. They were fine when they were relieving their pangs of guilt with their contributions and their participation in the panels and the forum groups, but now that it has come down to the stark reality, when it becomes a matter of putting into practice what you've discussed in your forums and panels, you've got a lot of hang-ups."

Mrs. Chisholm views with more than mild suspicion that current catchword, black capitalism. "What is black capitalism?" she says with something between a laugh and a sneer. "A tax-incentive plan for white businessmen? How many black entrepreneurs can they create? The focus must be on the masses of black people who realistically *we know* can never become capitalists. The focus *must* be on massive manpower training. Mr. Roy Innis of CORE is rounding up support for his so-called 'Community self-determination' bill, and I expect that Mr. James Farmer will probably be its champion in Washington. This is not a bill I think I will support. Just wait, there may be some fireworks."

In her first, combustive, getting-acquainted weeks in Washington, Mrs. Chisholm has been an instant celebrity on Capitol Hill. As she hurries down a corridor or boards an escalator in her spindly high-heeled shoes and longish skirts, she smiles left and right to those who invariably recognize her. Black maintenance men are treated to a special, warm hello; women secretaries nudge each other and nod happily in her direction. Once inside the leathery, masculine House chamber, she sits regally in her chair, at attention. "That's the woman who beat what's his name," remarked one visitor to the Congressional galleries. In these early weeks, Mrs. Chisholm has made news—and has made the rounds of public functions, party meetings, speaking engagements and televised interviews on the kind of schedule a Mrs. Roosevelt would find exhausting. The demands on her time that come back from her being the nation's "first black woman Congressman" show no sign of letting up, nor does she seem willing or able to call a halt.

A few weeks ago in Brooklyn, two old friends of Shirley Chisholm were talking about the woman they knew and the public figure—"the national figure"—she has become. As Chisholm-watchers they speculated about what Shirley will do next. "If she buckles down and concentrates on her legislative work, it will be wonderful," one said. "If they turn her into a symbol, if she just does the ceremonial things, or just goes around making speeches and doing very little else— then it will really be disappointing." So far Shirley Chisholm has seldom disappointed.

I'M A PEOPLE'S POLITICIAN

INTERVIEW BY MIRIAM ROSEN
PACIFICA RADIO
JUNE 1972

MIRIAM ROSEN: The first thing that I wanted to talk to you about is the program that you have, because very few people talk about it. And I see that you even have sheets—position papers that you have put out—and I just wanted to know how you went about creating your platform.

SHIRLEY CHISHOLM: For four years, I was a member of the New York State Legislature, and then for the past three years a member of the United States Congress. And I've had an opportunity to assess and evaluate, by the voluminous correspondence that was sent to my state legislative office and then later my congressional office, as to what the needs and the hopes and the concerns are, in the minds of the American people. So over a period of time, whether on a state or a national level, one begins to be able to piece together the kinds of things that the American people want to see their representatives move in the direction of.

So this year when I decided to make a bid for the presidency, I went back over all of my notes and all of the concerns that have been shared with me via letters from people, not only in my own state but all over this country. And I also began to listen to some of the gentlemen who had indicated that they would be interested in running for the presidency of this country. And on the basis of some of the things that they were saying, I began to put together my thirteen position papers. And believe it or not, I was the first person running for this office that sent these papers out to the newspapers, the media. Papers on law and justice in our country—consumerism, housing, education, women's rights, day care centers—papers on the domestic concerns of the American people.

And I have had to spend so much time during the past seven months, while I've been out here defending why I am running for the presidency of this country, the people, who now have recognized and have seen my position papers, realize, that I am truly a person. Let's forget the woman or man bit. Truly a person with depth, with capacity and solutions to problems in this country. In fact, when people saw me for the first time three weeks ago on the three networks after I won that suit,* the letters that came into my office in terms of the fact that people said, "Why, you have more sense than some of the rest of them put together, where have you been"—it's unfortunate, but because I am Black, simultaneously a woman, both of these things wrapped into one, it has been the most difficult thing to get the American people directed to what I've been talking about.

---

* Chisholm filed suits against the three major networks, the National Broadcasting Company, the Columbia Broadcasting System, and the American Broadcasting Company, on the grounds that they denied her television time equal to that scheduled for Senators Hubert H. Humphrey of Minnesota and George McGovern of South Dakota before the June 6 primaries in California and New Jersey.

When you hear George Wallace talking about the tax reform, so much of what George is saying came right out of my position papers! So much of what [Hubert] Humphrey has been saying came out of my position papers—I recognize the words, and the putting together the sentences! But they are *serious* candidates. Shirley Chisholm is not serious. So Shirley Chisholm never got the projection that she needed to get. It was a wonderful thing that I won that ballot, with the FCC, about three weeks ago. If not, the American people would never really have known that I am a woman, and I'm not trying to boast at all, but I am a woman with ability and with intelligence and with depth. That is the sadness about this country. And that's why I made my mind up that I was going to stay in this race come thick or thin. And I was going to go all the way to Miami because even though the papers have been underscoring me, even though many people have been saying, well she can't be serious—they're going to see me in action at the National Convention. And I mean this. I am committed to this. As an instrument of people in this country who've been left out. An instrument of people whose councilman advice has never been sought in terms of putting a ticket together, only using the people every four years for their votes.

I look at all of these distinguished senators telling all of the people what they're going to do for women, what they're going to do for blacks, what they're going to do for Chicanos, what they're going to do for this group and the other group. Oh darn it, they've been in the United States Senate for ten or more years—if they had a concern about the American Indian, they would have done something already about the miserable living conditions that those Indians live on, in terms of the reservations where 70 percent of them don't live to see the age of forty. They don't have a concern about women! They don't have a concern about the conservation and preservation of human resources! They're only interested in these human resources every four years when it's time to go out and get the vote.

And that's why, when people say, "Oh what makes you so different from all the rest of them," I say, "I am different. Because I have a gut commitment to people first of all." All of the rest of them have a commitment to different interest groups, financial groups, power groups—I'm espoused only by a lot of folks in this country who told me they didn't want to vote between the lesser of the two evils anymore. They wanted to give their vote to somebody that they knew deep down within themselves had a commitment to people, and for whatever that vote would mean, at least it would give me that much more added strength that I need when I get to the convention.

ROSEN: I saw an ad in the *Village Voice* that referred to you as "[fellow candidate George] McGovern's conscience" and then I heard you call yourself "the shaker-upper of the system, within the system," so I'd like you to talk a little bit about . . . about that role that you've taken on, because a lot of people are saying, you know, what is that woman trying to do, and I think that that deals with the issue.

CHISHOLM: Many people don't understand that when you're going to bring about change in a society, that change has to come from those individuals who have a really deep commitment to what they're doing—and not only have a deep commitment to what they're doing but to be able to withstand the stresses and the strains that will come from people misinterpreting your actions. Because I am not a traditional candidate. I am not a white person and I am not a male person. I am a part of two segments of America who have never had any real solid input in terms of running for the highest office of this land.

People are going to say "what is she trying to do" because they don't seem to understand that people like myself, and many others, are sick and tired of hearing about the multifacetedness of the American dream. They don't seem to understand that what I am doing is trying to chart a course or open up the whole process to other kinds of Americans who have never had the opportunity to aspire for the highest office in this land. So therefore, people who are not deep thinkers, and people who don't understand what a person like myself is doing, is going to always say "what is she trying to do." Because it's much better in a society to go along with whatever is happening, and when a person like myself dares to move beyond the realm of the traditional way of doing things, people either think you're half crazy, or they think that you have a real lust for power, or they think all kinds of things about you.

But then if you go back in history, all of the persons who have brought about changes in society, for the most part, have been individuals who very much have been alone, have had to be lonely because they've always been ahead of their time. I am a shaker-upper of the system within the system! Because there are lots of Americans, black and white, who tell me straight, "You can't do it, Shirley. The system is not the kind of system that's going to be responsive to Indians, to Black people, to poor whites in the same way that it has been responsive to those who have been controlling the resources of this country—you can't do it!" And I have said, "Well, I want to accept the challenge, to see if all of those of us who have been so helpless and so powerless cannot come together at a national convention and withhold throwing support to certain individuals who want to get across the top until they deal with us in terms of what our demands and aspirations are going to be." And that's what I have been doing.

I know that it will be difficult for me to become president of these United States, but I also know that those of us who just sit back, and just give up, and just mumble and grumble—those individuals are not going to bring about change either! So either you decide that you are going to take a challenge head-on, such as I am doing, or you're going to become so completely withdrawn from the system that you're going to say it's no use. I don't choose to take that latter course. I choose to still fight and believe, really believe, that we can make it responsive. That doesn't say what's going to happen to me in terms of the future. Will I be able to continue this way of changing do not come about I don't know, but I'm willing to accept the challenge and try to do it.

ROSEN: Well if you're McGovern's conscience, how did you feel when he put his advertisement in the *Wall Street Journal* and started making statements that sounded like he was conceding a little bit to big business, that he was a little bit worried about losing the support of big business.

CHISHOLM: Well, I've always said over and over again that I'm the only candidate out here that is espoused by the people and comes from the people. But I haven't had labor interests or banking interests or corporate interests or oil depletion interests or military-industrial complex interests give me a dime. And whether McGovern, Humphrey, or anybody wants to admit it or not, in the scheme of American presidential politics, he who pays the piper calls the tune. And that is why the American people distrust their politicians, and this is why I keep telling the American people, "Yes, I'm a politician." But I am a different breed of politician that is emerging—that is why it's so hard for many Americans to really understand "what is she up to" because I don't fit the traditional mold. I don't play the game cozily like it's supposed to be played. I don't wheel and deal and have conferences with the big bosses and the big officials. I cross all those lines and I go directly to the people. I'm a people's politician. Now McGovern—with all due respect, he's a decent, honorable man. But McGovern is not as free as Shirley Chisholm is, and he knows it and I know it.

ROSEN: But if you're going to be tugging on his left arm, and business is going to be tugging on his right arm, where is that going to leave the people. That's what I'm getting at. I see what you're trying to do—you're trying to create a space but business, or whatever, is trying to maintain a space. How is that going to be fought out?

CHISHOLM: Well, I don't think you're gonna fight anything out easily or bring it to a conclusion at this particular election.

I really don't. But I think, really, what is happening is that I've already had an impact on America. And I know this on the basis of my travels, that people are asking certain questions of Humphrey, McGovern, all of them; they see them after I have come into their community. I've gotten to the point where I have Humphrey and McGovern talking about Mexican-Americans in their cabinets and they didn't say that at the beginning of seven months ago. But Shirley Chisholm has been saying this over and over, so this is pricking the conscience. All I can say is that I'm a shaker-upper. That's exactly what I am.

ROSEN: Where do you have slates in New York right now?

CHISHOLM: I have slates in Eighteenth, Nineteenth, and Twentieth Congressional Districts in Manhattan. That's in the East Side area, the Harlem area, and East Harlem area—Eighteenth, Nineteenth, and Twentieth. I have two slates in Brooklyn, in the Eleventh and Twelfth Congressional Districts, and I have in the Twenty-Third Congressional District, Bronx, and a part of Westchester. And I just couldn't run delegates in every district because, as you know, I don't have that kind of money.

MINORITY STUDENTS AT RISK

INTERVIEW BY LARRY KEETER
JOURNAL OF DEVELOPMENTAL EDUCATION
JANUARY 1987

Former Congresswoman Shirley Chisholm holds the Purington Chair of Anthropology and Sociology at Mount Holyoke College, the oldest women's college in America. She recently spoke at Appalachian State University on "Women and Minorities as Policymakers in the U.S.: A Contemporary Perspective." She also led a faculty-student seminar on "The Minority Student at Risk: The Effects of Racism on the College Campus." —Larry Keeter, 1987

LARRY KEETER: Professor Chisholm, we have recently heard reports that the number of minority students, and particularly the number of black students, is decreasing on American college campuses. From your background and experience, why is this happening?

SHIRLEY CHISHOLM: The first factor at work here is the economic period we now face. The fathers of many, many black families are out of work. These men were recent arrivals in the workforce who became part of the "last hired, last fired" syndrome in spite of their business, technical or academic training.

A good many of these men, too, were making from $25,000 to $50,000 per year, and some of their sons and daughters were enrolled in private black institutions that cost from $10,000 to $14,000 per year. If a father paid 50 to 55 percent of his child's tuition and fees but became unemployed, the student has no choice but to drop out of college, for no school, black or white, can pick up that amount of slack. We see this kind of dropping out going on all over this country, and it's very much tied to the economic picture of blacks.

KEETER: Does that mean, then, that if we are to improve access to education for blacks and other minorities, then we must further address the economic aspects of black students' lives? There is a belief on some campuses that black students are being coddled; some students feel that way, and to a surprising degree, so do some administrations and faculty. These people believe that black students already get preferential treatment and financial aid. What can be done about this pervasive attitude?

CHISHOLM: Oh, I know that, yes I do. Whether people want to recognize it or not, the overwhelming majority of minority students come from the bottom of the nation's economic scale. Their families are at or below the poverty line. They are consistently and persistently at the bottom because of historical and economic reasons.

The financial aid programs, on the other hand, were set up to help those at the bottom of the economic scale. So these students' family incomes fit into the financial aid formula more readily than do those of white students. And I don't argue with the way the financial aid works out to support black students. We need mechanisms that will help overcome their backgrounds, or it may never happen.

People need to understand that this has nothing to do with preferential treatment. Let's say we have two students: Sally, a white student, and Tom, a black student. Whose family has the highest income? Overall, and generally speaking, Sally's family makes more money than Tom's, so Tom receives more financial aid. It's a simple matter of economics. And if the financial aid is cut, as the current administration wants, who is more likely to drop out of school? Tom is; Sally's family is much more likely to be able to make up for the lost financial aid. It's an issue of economics, not an issue of race.

KEETER: How can the colleges and universities better serve these students to succeed academically and socially? What kind of climate and educational programs can we develop that will provide better support for minority students?

CHISHOLM: Colleges and universities, as institutions, can certainly help minority students cope with their new environment. During the first or second week of classes, the president or the vice presidents should call every freshman student into a large auditorium and lay out some policies in a way that students will understand, and make it clear that each student is there to get an education. This leader must state very carefully and specifically how the minority students will be treated on campus, how the white students will be treated on campus, and then impress students that this is important to the life of the school.

A person at the top must let the freshmen know that racist attitudes and actions will not be tolerated on the campus and that one group will not be favored over another. There should be a grievance system to handle complaints from students and give redress for any wrongs. The tone must be set by a top administrator who makes clear the expectations set forth by the institution. And no milquetoast about it!

KEETER: This could be part of freshman orientation.

CHISHOLM: Yes, it needs to be done early. I've seen college campuses festering with racism, and some administrators just closing their eyes to it. It's an uncomfortable issue, and they just hope it will go away. But it doesn't go away—it gets worse. As I see it, the top administration must take an active role.

There are three or four other things that can be done, too. I've thought about this for a long time, and I believe that one of the most important actions is that colleges and universities mandate certain courses which must be taken by all students. One of those courses should be the history of black people. It's very important for whites to learn this kind of information; when people understand the development of a situation, have some knowledge and background to apply to understanding it, they have more tolerance. Mandating the course is important, because given the choice, few white students will take black history or a black studies course.

Secondly, the colleges must diligently encourage black and white students to stop isolating themselves from each other. Students need joint programs; right now we have a black studies club, or the Harriet Tubman Society or an

Italian club, lots of groups on campus. These serve to reinforce the members and provide certain kinds of support to them, of course, but there must also be opportunities on campus for students to mingle. I think this should be arranged by representatives of different groups; if it doesn't happen, the hostility, misunderstandings, skepticism, and suspicions continue to grow. Isolated groups create a sense of psychological security for the participants, but these groups prevent people from getting to know each other as human beings. College and university administrators are in wonderful positions to call upon student leaders and work out ways that these groups can get together and get to know each other better.

Third, I think there should be different kinds of ways that black and white students can have contact. For example, during Black History Week, the university could sponsor a black history contest, with prizes and awards. Both black and whites could participate. This also fosters not only knowledge of black history but a sense of healthy competition.

Minority students also drop out because they're not able to keep up with their studies. For quite some time now, colleges and universities have failed to budget a fair and reasonable percentage of money for remedial and tutorial programs. Now, I understand that the business of the university is to educate those students who are ready to do college-level work. If the money is limited, which it certainly is nowadays, the university cannot use it to do that which should have been done in high school; money can't be spent for massive tutorial and remediation programs when budgets are slashed across the board. It's a hard decision, because when students are not able to get additional help, they fall behind and then drop out. Many minority students need extra help, they fall behind and then drop out. Many minority students need extra help with reading and writing skills and other subjects, and they tell me that they're not getting the help they need.

What I want is for people to forget about skin color and get students to interact. Right now, black and white students on college campuses are not interacting; they're suspicious and skeptical of each other. Some black students don't even want to talk to white students, and vice versa, because their peer groups wouldn't like it. That's madness!

You know, this is a very hate-filled society. The colleges and universities must become aware of the kinds of problems and situations that tend to polarize and alienate black and white students. The administration of the postsecondary institution must take the lead and set the tone for the students. Solving these problems must be an ongoing effort: We must try to do something about the problem, then reassemble and talk about the results, and try again.

KEETER: In your experience, are there faculty behaviors that alienate black students or communicate uneasiness? Do faculty sometimes communicate that they have different expectations of black students?

CHISHOLM: I think this is a very important question. Black students have many insecurities and anxieties, and they aren't at all sure that people really like them. This also applies, to some extent, to dealings with black faculty. Whites—along with blacks—must realize that the era of beneficent paternalism is over. Blacks have become very sensitive, and rightly so, about attitudes of overprotectiveness or someone's bending over backwards to accommodate them.

Most blacks would rather that you be direct with them about your feelings. Don't worry about upsetting a black student or faculty member any more than you worry about upsetting anyone else. State the facts, state the case. You're man to man, you're woman to woman. Black students are not little children who need special handling so as not to hurt their feelings.

You see, pain is not new to these students, or to these faculty; they've been hurt most of their lives by the society in which they must grow. At the same time they resent this beneficent paternalism. Many whites don't know how to cope with blacks; and they feel uneasy about communicating to individual blacks or a group. I believe that the best approach is simply to be yourself. Be yourself! That's the best way.

KEETER: We have studies that show that there's a pervasive silence about the subject of racism on college campuses, especially in the classroom. Why is this silence so uniform? Some say that if you visit American classrooms today, you would think racism no longer exists because nobody talks about it anymore.

CHISHOLM: That's human nature: Some people think that if you don't talk about a thing, it will go away. That's always happened in our society, and it's a natural human reaction. And people think racism was taken care of in the 1960s.

KEETER: Do *you* think racism is no longer a problem?

CHISHOLM: Of course racism is still a serious problem; what's changed is attitudes toward it. I hear people say, "Let's not talk any more about racism or sexism. Things aren't like they were twenty years ago. Let's talk about something else." Nobody wants to open up Pandora's box again; we all had enough of Pandora's box in the 1960s.

KEETER: How can we help college and university faculty to encourage frank discussion of racial topics in the classroom? I think most faculty members are reluctant to discuss racism, yet you're saying that colleges and universities must take an active role in addressing the issue.

CHISHOLM: I don't think it's very successful to deal with the topic directly. It wouldn't be best for a faculty member to announce that today the class will talk about sexism, and tomorrow slavery, and the next day racism. It would be much better to use parables or special stories as a basis for discussion of these issues. Faculty could use personal experience or a short article or story as a point of departure. I use this approach in my studies of black women in America.

KEETER: What makes this approach work for students?

CHISHOLM: Everybody likes a good story, you know, especially if it's told by a good storyteller. And students are curious. After I tell a story, I ask them how they saw it, what hit them about the story. They begin to open up, and they get drawn in, sometimes unknowingly, to the issues facing blacks. A good story can catch the imagination, the student's fantasy, and become a basis for a lesson.

One of the issues we discuss in my classes is why black women are not as interested in the women's movement in this country as white women are. When an instructor is in control of the classroom situation, she can say things that are sure to provoke reactions from students. I might say, for example, during this discussion, "Oh, black women have not been so enthusiastic about the women's movement because they know that while white women are not always treated as they should be, at least they have the commonality of being white. Black women see the priority of race over sex as the important thing." Then I am able to lead the class back into the history of the black people and help the class understand that anything that pulls black women away from solidarity with black men is seen as troublesome. My next controversial statement might be, "So that's why black women have always been stronger than white women." And students leap to that, saying, "What do you mean by that, Mrs. Chisholm?"

I like this indirect way of provoking thought. It gets students' attention, and it starts discussions. The instructor stays in control and can keep coming back to the topic.

KEETER: There's another form of racism that I've heard about on various campuses. Minority students have mentioned it, and they say it happens frequently. They call it the "hate stare." Do you know about this? Students say that it's a look that whites use to let blacks know that they're in the whites' "territory" or to create general discomfort. Have you seen this happening?

CHISHOLM: Yes, I have, and it's very annoying to me, even though I'm a fairly mature person. There's a variant, too, of the hate stare: The whites will walk right past you and then laugh at you.

KEETER: Laugh as though there were something ridiculous about you?

CHISHOLM: No, it's an arrogant laugh, one that says they detest you. This doesn't happen when the white person walks by alone; it happens when two or three or more are together. It's a form of expressing racism, and it happens to me once in a while even now.

On the other hand, black students roll their eyes if white students upset or annoy them. Have you noticed that? It's a way of showing displeasure, detestation, or a kind of veiled hostility. All students, you know, are human beings, and they all have their different and individual ways of reacting to situations.

KEETER: This hate stare and these snide laughs must surely influence the black students' perceptions of themselves. Even though all whites don't treat black students that way, is there a tendency for the blacks to think that people regard them as unwelcome in the classroom or elsewhere on campus?

CHILSHOLM: Oh, yes. Have you noticed that black students are reluctant to speak up in class? Many are afraid of being ridiculed in the classroom like they are outside of it, so they keep quiet. You'd be surprised—many black students feel this way.

KEETER: What are the family pressures on black students? It would seem that when the family at home is making sacrifices to send the child to college and doing without to keep her there, the guilt load must be tremendous.

CHISHOLM: Some black students drop out of college because they can't deal with this pressure. They experience pressure from their peers and pressures from their families reminding them that they're maybe the first one in the family ever to go to college, that they've got to succeed, that everyone at home is doing without so the student can be educated. "Don't fool around in college, don't you come back here with bad grades, don't you come back here pregnant, don't you get in with a bad crowd, don't get on drugs." The students want to carry home good grades and do well in college, but some just break under the relentless pressure.

KEETER: That sounds like extra pressure that the average white, middle-class student might not experience.

CHISHOLM: That's right. Every college student faces academic pressures, but minority students face the social pressures resulting from being different and highly visible. Students who aren't strong, who lack self-confidence, face a very difficult struggle. For instance, we've recently been hearing references to the idea that the black race is an inferior race. Students who are feeling inadequate within themselves can really break down when faced with such statements. I've seen students go to pieces under this kind of pressure.

KEETER: We've spoken about the difficulties that black students have on campus, but what about their strengths? I've personally observed that minority students exhibit some strengths that definitely contribute to their success. What kind of strengths do these students develop when they persevere and have commitment and adaptability?

CHISHOLM: Some black students are very knowledgeable about the goals and objectives of which they are a part. They don't come to school to socialize or be friendly; they come to get an education. These students don't have time to worry about what white students say to them or about them or the way somebody looks at them. The black peers of these students may be very negative toward them also, for different reasons. The students I'm talking about tend to be the intellectually oriented ones who have great resilience in remaining committed to their goals through the difficulties they experience, and these students are very strong.

Another kind of strength that black students bring to college is family loyalty and support. Now I know I've talked about family pressure, but families can also be very supportive. In black families, aunts and uncles and grandparents often contribute to the child's education. These students are very conscious of the hopes and expectations of their families, and they want to meet those expectations and succeed. This is a kind of family loyalty that gives black students the comfort and strength to get through college.

KEETER: I've heard you speak of the strength and commitment you've felt because of your upbringing, and how you survived and maintained your commitment and developed your intellect because of your experiences.

CHISHOLM: Yes, I am what I am because of the environment in which I was reared. I was born in this country but grew up in Barbados in the West Indies. My parents returned to America for two purposes: to buy a home for the family, and to give their four daughters a good education. While we were being reared in the islands, we went to school under the British system, which was very highly disciplined. We were reading and writing at ages three and four, and our parents and teachers collaborated to keep us in line. We couldn't come home from school and complain that the teacher smacked us because Grandmother would give an additional scolding or another smack. Everybody worked together to mold us in preparation of the future. I doubt I would have accomplished what I have in this country if I had not had that kind of discipline; it was an important part of my life.

My grandmother often told me, "Excellence, child, excellence! Not mediocrity. The world is filled with mediocre individuals." Oh, if I could hear that old lady again—these things were deeply embedded in me, and at a very early age I developed confidence in myself.

When I returned to America, I attended junior high

and high school. I was a tiny little thing, and the principal couldn't understand how this little black girl had such spunk. I asked questions in school without feeling ashamed or embarrassed. In fact, I became somewhat of a nuisance, they thought.

I didn't know what a nuisance was; I'd been taught that if you don't know about something, *ask*. If you don't understand the answers, ask for an explanation. Was I shy? I didn't know the meaning of the word. These were my strengths.

KEETER: That's certainly evident. I've heard people comment that you have such confidence, that you will say, before God and your conscience, exactly what's on your mind.

CHISHOLM: Yes, I've always been like that, and that's part of the reason I was a problem to the politicians. They knew I would raise my hand, ask the question, and be unafraid. I'm not afraid of anything or anybody—no, not at all. The worst that will happen is that someone will tell me No—and I understand that.

KEETER: Thanks, Mrs. Chisholm, for giving us your time and the benefit of your experience.

THE LAST INTERVIEW

INTERVIEW BY CAMILLE COSBY
NATIONAL VISIONARY LEADERSHIP PROJECT
MAY 7, 2002

CAMILLE COSBY: Ms. Chisholm, where and when were you born?

SHIRLEY CHISHOLM: I was born in New York, on November 30th, 1924.

COSBY: Did you grow up in New York?

CHISHOLM: No, I did not grow up in New York. I left New York at the age of three and grew up on the island of Barbados in the British West Indies.

COSBY: One of your parents was brought up or lived in Barbados?

CHISHOLM: My mother was born in Barbados and my father was born in British Guyana.

COSBY: Oh, I see.

CHISHOLM: So both of them married and of course, I'm of Caribbean heritage, therefore.

COSBY: What was your childhood like in Barbados?

CHISHOLM: Oh, my childhood, I can remember it. It . . . it was exciting. We live on a great big farm and we had to take care of all of the animals on the farm—the chickens, the goats, the sheep, the hens, all of the animals on the farm. And I'll never forget, whenever it rained, and the weather was very, very bad, my responsibility was to go out and really bring the animals into the shade, and I became afraid of lightning because of that.

COSBY: Really?

CHISHOLM: Because whenever I went out to bring the animals in, the lightning would be flashing sometimes, and whenever I get, would go to look at the animals, they would be stiff, they would be standing. And by the time I went over to pick them up and tried to bring them in, they would be dead. And that came from the lightning. The, the lightning was very, very fierce in the West Indies, and from then, even until today, I am scared to death of lightning.

COSBY: Well, apparently you had a lot of freedom on an island such as that. I mean, certainly, you could have freedom of movement, probably it was a communal environment. Is that what you experienced, and, and were you living with someone in the family?

CHISHOLM: I grew up with my maternal grandmother, and my maternal aunt, and my maternal uncle. I went there at the age of three, and I went to the elementary schools in the islands. I did not return to the United States until nine years of age. So I had six years upbringing in the island of Barbados.

COSBY: Fantastic. Good for you. Are you one of several siblings?

CHISHOLM: Yes, I am. I'm the oldest of four girls, and all of us, we received our elementary school in the islands, and I don't know if this is important or not, but all three of us got scholarships because we were so bright and we had very high IQs. And that is attributable to my rearing in the British West Indies.

COSBY: I see. Because you feel that the school system is superior.

CHISHOLM: Oh, yeah, the school system was fantastic.

COSBY: I see.

CHISHOLM: Really fantastic.

COSBY: Very good. Also, probably because you were in such a supportive environment, that always encourages learning as well.

CHISHOLM: Of course.

COSBY: What was your parents' economic level?

CHISHOLM: My father was an unskilled laborer, and my mother was a domestic for many, many years. This is why she took us to the West Indies, so that the six years that I grew up in the West Indies, my mom returned to the United States and was a seamstress and took in a lot of sewing for people so she can earn money, and helped my father to get a lot of money, hopefully to buy a home. And that's what they did. This is why my mother took us there, so that we would grow up with my grandparents, and she would come back to the United States of America and work side by side with my father in order to increase the income and eventually buy a home for us, and that's what happened.

COSBY: Oh. So during those years, from age three to nine years of age, your parents were busy working and saving their money to build their home.

CHISHOLM: Uh-huh.

COSBY: I understand that your father was a Garveyite, and was your mother as well?

CHISHOLM: No, no, no. My mother always used to tell Dad, "Look. Charles, don't discuss that with me." My mother was very stern. She said, "I am not interested in any political stuff." [*Laughter*]

CHISHOLM: But my father was an ardent Garveyite, and my father—I think that's where I got my interest in politics, from Dad, because Dad used to take me to the meetings with him, even though I was a child then of ten, eleven years of age. I used to get excited.

COSBY: For those of us who don't know who Marcus Garvey is, would you just give us some background on him and what a Garveyite is.

CHISHOLM: Yeah. Marcus Garvey was a Jamaican who believed that blacks should return to Africa and build up Africa and accept Africa as their home. And he led a movement, here, in the United States, and he got caught up in a lot of scandal, and, eventually, it collapsed, and that was that.

COSBY: Do you think that your father's involvement in Marcus Garvey's movement had any impact on your development?

CHISHOLM: Oh, yes. Because I read everything I could about Marcus Garvey, and my father was such an ardent Garveyite that he would talk about him all the time. Yes.

COSBY: Fantastic. You are a child of immigrant parents from the Caribbean. Was it difficult for your family to fit in the New York City community that they lived in, in your youth?

CHISHOLM: No, I don't think so because at that particular time many people from abroad were coming in, people from

Italy and Spain—all over. So my parents were part of that movement that was taking place at that time in the United States of America.

COSBY: I see. Okay. You had scholarships to Vassar and to Oberlin.

CHISHOLM: Uh-huh.

COSBY: Why did you choose to go to Brooklyn College?

CHISHOLM: My parents didn't have the money to buy the nice clothing. I'll never forget that. And my mother said to me, "Shirley, I think that you should go to Brooklyn College," because it was near to my home. I could travel by bus, and I didn't have to lay out a great deal of money in terms of buying special kinds of clothing. So that's why.

I was very sad when I learned I couldn't go to Vassar, because I really wanted to go to Vassar College.

COSBY: That was your first choice.

CHISHOLM: Yes, that was my first choice.

COSBY: I see. And did you do any graduate work after you graduated from Brooklyn College?

CHISHOLM: Yes. I went on to Columbia University and received a degree in, a master's degree in, early childhood education. And then I went on further and received a certificate as a supervisor in the field of education.

COSBY: And why did you choose education?

CHISHOLM: I always loved being around children and working with children, always, from the time I was a tot.

COSBY: Before entering politics, you had devoted yourself to the needs of children and you just said you love children. What brought you to that choice? You said you've always loved being around children.

CHISHOLM: I think it was due to the fact that I used to watch my mother with my younger sisters, and part of my responsibility, even though I was so young, was to also help take care of my sisters. And I just developed a kind of maternalistic—let me use that word—maternalistic attitude towards my sisters.

COSBY: I see.

CHISHOLM: And I used to love to put them to bed and coach them. I just really loved being with children.

COSBY: So you always felt responsibilities—because you were the eldest, you are the eldest of your siblings—and you felt that you had to take care of them and be responsible.

CHISHOLM: That's correct.

COSBY: How was it for your first husband, Conrad Chisholm, when you became more involved in your political aspirations; how did others treat him, particularly men?

CHISHOLM: Oh, in fact, they didn't pay much attention to him. Everything was Shirley, Shirley. The limelight was on Shirley, and this was one of the reasons why my first marriage cracked up after twenty-four years, because they put my husband in a position of becoming extremely jealous.

COSBY: I see.

CHISHOLM: He became very, very jealous, and I could understand, because no attention was being paid to him. And everything was Shirley, Shirley, Shirley this, Shirley that. And then there was, "He is the husband of Shirley Chisholm." And you can imagine what that does to a person's ego after a while.

And so that was the thing that really led to the breakup of my marriage, this business of his being jealous, and everybody—everybody catering to his wife, Shirley.

COSBY: Because you, apparently, you needed to have someone who was very . . . because you definitely were a trailblazer at that time.

CHISHOLM: Uh-huh, yes.

COSBY: So the pressures must have been great on him but also on you . . . on you to take a back step.

CHISHOLM: Yes, yes, yes.

COSBY: I see; okay. Before you successfully ran for the New York State Assembly in 1964, what did you do to prepare for your political journey?

CHISHOLM: I really didn't do anything, specially. I was always interested in politics. But I remember the turning point came when I was . . . I think I was a sophomore at Brooklyn College. And we had a political, our political leader, a white gentleman, Stanley Steingut—I'll never forget him—the leader of the district, came to give a lecture, and I remember so well, he said, "Black people are now moving ahead, but there's going to be one basic truth that you're going to have to accept, whether you want to or not. That black people cannot get ahead unless they have white people."

I remember that. That stuck with me, and I said to myself, uh-huh, that's what you think! And it was a challenge from that time on. That, that really had an impact on me.

COSBY: But, you know, Ms. Chisholm, you seem to have so much tenacity. Where do you think that came from, I mean, to even take on that kind of attitude?

CHISHOLM: It came from my grandmother. My grandmother had a fantastic influence in my life. She would always check my homework, and she would, each night she would say, "Repeat it to me." And if I didn't stand up straight, she said, "Child"—this is the way she'd talk—"Child, you got to stand up straight, let the world see you coming." And I would have to stand up straight. I think that's why I'm so erect—[*laughter*]

CHISHOLM: And she would say, "And don't slur your words." She, oh, she was pushy. My grandmother—I would say that my granny had the greatest influence in my life. And then along came, when I came back to this country, two other women that influenced me a great deal—Mary McLeod Bethune. She said to me, "You're smart, you're a very smart girl, but you must stand and fight." I'll never forget her words. "You must fight. You must fight." And the other woman who had a fantastic influence was Eleanor Roosevelt.

COSBY: Really?

CHISHOLM: Eleanor Roosevelt came to New York City and I was in a, a contest, a debating contest, and I won the debate in the whole city of New York. And she said to me, I'll never forget this tall woman, her hair in a chignon, and this little porkpie hat on, and she was ugly. She was very ugly. But Eleanor, the moment she opened her mouth, you felt a warmth. It was beautiful.

And she said to me, "Shirley St. Hill"— that is my maiden name—"Shirley St. Hill, you're very smart, you're intelligent. You must fight. You must get up and don't let anybody stay in your way; even a woman can do it."

COSBY: Wow. Well, it sounds like you had three very important women in your life.

CHISHOLM: Definitely.

COSBY: Your grandmother, your mother, Mary McLeod Bethune. Well, the fourth one would be, of course, Mrs. Roosevelt. That's very interesting. And how fortunate for you.

CHISHOLM: Uh-huh.

COSBY: And then, of course, you had your father being a Garveyite.

CHISHOLM: A Garveyite, yes.

COSBY: Yes. Fantastic. But then you, because prior to your political career, you, I understand, taught nursery school and then you became supervisor of a network of nursery schools?

CHISHOLM: Yes.

COSBY: Do you think that what you learned as a supervisor, as an administrator, helped you to be, to know how to organize politically, how to network, and all the other things that one needs to do to become a politician?

CHISHOLM: Oh, yes. It had a terrific impact. This is why, today, even my friends say to me, "Shirley, for God's sake, don't be so darn organized."

COSBY: Yes.

CHISHOLM: I acquired the organizational skills that I have in getting people together from those experiences, and for that I'm very, very thankful. Very thankful.

COSBY: Tell me something about that period when you were the supervisor for the network of nursery schools. Did you learn people skills at that time? Did you learn how to just interact with people, make them feel that they could trust you, or will you just, just describe that period a little bit.

CHISHOLM: Well, I would say two things. I read. There's nothing that makes me feel better than I have a book, and I read so much material on these different kinds of skills that were necessary: how to organize, how to get people together, how to talk to them, and talk with them. I received a lot of my skills just from reading.

COSBY: I understand that you did things like compiled voter lists, carried petitions, rung doorbells, manned the telephone. All those kinds of things that really is more of grassroots work.

CHISHOLM: Yes, yes; that's right.

COSBY: Yes. So all of that came in handy later on.

CHISHOLM: Oh, yes.

COSBY: Please explain the impact of New York's political clubs on developing local politicians.

CHISHOLM: Oh! [*laughter*]

CHISHOLM: New York, at that time, it was a situation in which the minorities had absolutely no pull. No one paid attention to the Hispanic peoples, to the black peoples. And the clubs, for, for the most part, were run by two particular ethnic groups: the Italians and the Irish. And that's how I got my first entrance into active politics, because I went into the club in my neighborhood, and my neighborhood was comprised primarily of Puerto Ricans and blacks.

COSBY: And you speak Spanish fluently, don't you?

CHISHOLM: Yes, I do. And this, this club was headed by an Irishman, and he wouldn't give the, the women a chance at a club to do anything. He wouldn't give the blacks and, and the Hispanic people an opportunity to do anything. And then I joined the club because I was already beginning to move up, politically. And I was very active in community groups, and what I did in community groups, I was always organizing groups. Organize, organize, organize.

And I raised my hand in the club, and I asked him one basic question. I said, "Mr. Carney, I think it's very important, that since you expect the women of this club to really raise money, money to go into the treasury in order to help the gentlemen run for political office, you don't have any women running. Don't you think it's about time that the gentlemen of the club, who put the money in the treasury of the club, give the women money to get the materials that they need for the club?"

And he said, "Order, order." And he was, he was very angry that I should raise this question, because it would mean we—we women—had to take money from our budgets and use it to buy pencils and paper and everything, and I was raising it, that the money should come out of the treasury.

And from that time, from the beginning of that little thing, my wings began to sprout all over the community. [*laughter*]

COSBY: Fantastic.

CHISHOLM: People said, "Gee, she's so brave, she—you know—she challenged Commissioner Carney last night, and he didn't know what to say." And that's how I began to move up, politically.

COSBY: Good for you, because certainly it is well-known that women have always done the work, but they don't get the credit.

CHISHOLM: That's right.

COSBY: But they do the work to put the men into office.

CHISHOLM: That's right. A lot of Irishwomen were in the club, and they said, "Shirley St. Hill, Shirley St. Hill—do it!"

COSBY: Yes!

CHISHOLM: "We'll follow you. We'll follow." And that's all I needed to hear. And they followed me, and that's how I began to move out and began to challenge the machine in the district, until I ran for the assembly and everything else. That's how I really sprouted my wings.

COSBY: I also understand that you formed a political club to put a very successful white lawyer into, I think, the State Assembly. Was that it?

CHISHOLM: Yes, yes.

COSBY: Okay. So that was one of your—

CHISHOLM: That was one of my—yes. And if anybody would ask me, well, what was the greatest thing that stood in your way of trying to really move up, politically? I would have to say men. [*laughter*]

CHISHOLM: White men, black men, Puerto Rican. Men!

COSBY: Men.

CHISHOLM: That's all. They gave me a hard time, because they said one thing about Shirley Chisholm, she's too darn outspoken, and she's always raising questions. She never keeps quiet. And what happened in the neighborhood, you heard it from the white men, the Puerto Rican men, the black men—all had their own little caucuses to decide to get together and see what we can do about this woman that's moving out called Shirley Chisholm.

COSBY: And what is the definition of being too outspoken?

CHISHOLM: Oh, God! Let's not talk about that! They tried to keep me, keep me down, keep me back. They used all kinds of tactics. But the thing about it—I was never afraid of men. Never afraid of men, and I think it was attributable to two things. I'm very friendly. I'm very outgoing. And I'm a person, I can laugh at myself and laugh at others. Very outspoken. And that's what—because I know the men, the black men in my community, they said we can't have a meeting—we don't even invite her to the meetings, and here she comes. She heard that we were having a meeting; she wanted to say hello. [*laughter*]

CHISHOLM: But it wasn't that. I knew that they were having a meeting and I wanted to invade their premises. [*laughter*]

CHISHOLM: You see? And find out what was going on. And I would—and, and when they saw me coming, they, they almost dropped dead. [*laughter*]

CHISHOLM: I really was not very nice in terms of how I had to react to them, but that, that was the only way I could react. That was the only way I could move out, because they wouldn't give me a chance, because they were afraid of my mouth.

COSBY: And afraid of change.

CHISHOLM: Yes.

COSBY: Yes, of course.

CHISHOLM: That was it. Yeah, that was it.

COSBY: And the influence you would have on other women—

CHISHOLM: Oh, the women. I brought the whole neighborhood behind me. That was the women. That's right.

COSBY: That is so interesting, how you remained so tenacious throughout that whole very difficult period, even in terms of what your first husband had to go through. Even in terms of the resistance from so many men. But there had to be some men who were supportive of you, too.

CHISHOLM: Oh, yes. Oh, yes, yes.

COSBY: So you had a healthy respect for men as well.

CHISHOLM: Yes. Oh, I love men. There's no doubt about it. Some of them, they usually think that I hated men; it wasn't that. It was a question of allowing and permitting women to come forth like everybody else.

COSBY: Yes.

CHISHOLM: You know? Don't tell me that I can't do it.

COSBY: Yes.

CHISHOLM: And I would, you know, I would say to somebody: What do you mean, telling me I can't do it? How do you know? [*laughter*]

CHISHOLM: You know, and, and they couldn't stand this, you know, this kind of retort.

COSBY: Do you think that, that the environment that you lived in for a short period of time, in Barbados, helped you to be persistent about your goals, and, and the support that you had from your family. Obviously, they said to you, you can do, you can be. Do you think that that helped you to just push through these obstacles?

CHISHOLM: Yes, I do. My life, those early years of my life on the island of Barbados, gave me the spirit, gave to me the spunk that was necessary to challenge all of these age-old traditions. And then, I was never afraid of anything, I was never afraid of anybody. And today, it's the same way. I'm not afraid of anything. I'm not afraid of anybody. You're going to hear from me. [*laughter*]

COSBY: With a smile on your face, right?

CHISHOLM: Yes. I always smile. [*laughter*]

COSBY: Very good. While in the State Assembly, you reversed a law that would badly affect female teachers. Please talk about that, as well as the CEK program, which you authored.

CHISHOLM: Well, I realized that the reason that black children were not getting along is because we didn't have access to scholarships, and I was determined that, while I was in the assembly, that I would have to work in the field of education. And so I brought this program in, CEK, Church, Education, and Knowledge. It was a battle, but I won it. I won it, and black youth were able to get scholarships, and black youth were able to move out.

And I felt very strongly, in looking around me in the neighborhood, and to see all of the black youth not having the same opportunities as the white youth did, because of the fact that they were going to inferior schools, inferior kinds of schools, that this is very important to me.

And so while I was in the assembly, I worked a great deal in the field of education.

COSBY: And, of course, that is your background, anyway. You have your master's degree in administration.

CHISHOLM: Yes, that was my master's, that's right.

COSBY: And then the, the female teachers. I understand that what you worked on was to enable them to have tenure while they were on maternity leave.

CHISHOLM: Yes. Teachers were so upset. They go on maternity leave and nobody does anything. You know, you go, you come back, you don't have your job. So I fought that and I won that. But that was—oh, that was a terrible, terrible battle. But I, I won, because—one thing about me, as you say—I'm a very tenacious person. I hold on. I really do hold on.

COSBY: No matter what.

CHISHOLM: Yes, yes. That's right. Hold on, no matter what. Uh-huh.

COSBY: Ms. Chisholm, how was New York's Twelfth District created in 1968?

CHISHOLM: You know, every ten years, when you have the census, there's a redistricting because of population changes, and it was created as a result of the work in the New York State Legislature at that time. And that's how I got the opportunity to move out to run for the Congress.

COSBY: Now, were you the first black to run for Congress, or the first black woman?

CHISHOLM: The first black woman to make the bid.

COSBY: Okay. And then your opponent was James Farmer, who led the Congress of Racial Equality during the civil rights movement. He was male and famous. You were female and you were not known nationally.

CHISHOLM: Yes.

COSBY: How did you beat him?

CHISHOLM: Well, James Farmer, he felt so sorry for me. He was a lovely man, though. We got along famously, because we both like to talk, and we would talk and exchange information and everything.

But James Farmer said to me, "Shirley, the Congress is not for you. We need strong people." And he used to use these adjectives. And he would come down on them. He said, "We need strong people. You're a little schoolteacher." [*laughter*]

COSBY: Little did he know . . .

CHISHOLM: Yes. And three things I think helped to bring him down, really. It was a bitter fight. One, he kept saying that that place is not a place for women. You need strong men. And I said, ah-ha, wait a minute. There are more women voters in my district.

COSBY: Yes.

CHISHOLM: And I used that. And boy, the women—white, black, Puerto Rican—all the women moved behind me.
And then another thing that insulted me. He would bring the trucks, with musicians on the trucks at the subway stations, and they would play the drums and the tom-toms and everything to give the idea of machismo and greatness. And this made me so angry.

So I said, you know, what I'm going to do with him. He lived in New York, downtown New York. So I hired some cameramen, and I say, for three weeks straight, watch James Farmer every time he comes out of his house, and then I reproduce it in auditoriums throughout the district. And they saw him come out, out of the, out of Manhattan to come into Brooklyn— [*laughter*]

CHISHOLM: —to run for Congress, and that helped to bring him down. And then he didn't know that I spoke Spanish. So when I would go into the Puerto Rican districts, and I'd say, "Senora, Sí Senora, escúchame!" Oh— [*laughter*]

CHISHOLM: His mouth fell open, and he said Lord, what else, what else is she going to bring to this race, you know? And that's how I did it, but we were good, yeah, we were good friends. But he said, "I could never understand—Shirley Chisholm, where do you get your nerve?" [*laughter*]

COSBY: Oh, fantastic. Then, in 1969, you were the first black woman, as you said earlier, elected to Congress. What was the mood of that Congress? That was the Ninety-Seventh Congress?

CHISHOLM: Yes.

COSBY: What was the mood? Because there were so many social movements going on at the time and had gone on in the civil rights movement; the Vietnam War was still going on. What was it like for you, in that Congress?

CHISHOLM: That was one of the most difficult moments of my life. For the first two to three months, I was miserable.

The gentlemen did not pay me any mind at all. When I would go to the lunchroom to eat, they would not sit at the same table as I did, because I was a black woman.

It was horrible, and I'll give you two little incidents that perhaps will show you that I had a sense of humor about a lot of things.

There was a little dining room beneath the floor of the House, and that was a place where we could go to get a bite if we were going to have a long day, and I did not know that in that dining room the tables were designated to the different delegations.

There was a table for New York, a table for Alabama, a table for—and I went one day to go down and sit at a table. I sat at a table 'cause nobody was sitting there. Ten chairs to the table, and I ordered my lunch. I was very hungry that day, and I got dessert and salad, and a little bit of everything put on the table. And I always took the *New York Times* and read it while I was eating, because nobody would sit by me.
So this day, I felt something hovering around me. I looked up, and if looks could kill, I would have been dead, because I was seated at the Georgia delegation table and didn't know it.

COSBY: Oh, my goodness! Of all tables.

CHISHOLM: I was at the Georgia delegation table and didn't know it. And this man stood up and looked at me, said, "You're sitting at the wrong table." I said, "What did you say?" He says, "I say, you're sitting at the wrong table." I said, "What table is this?" "Georgia delegation." "Oh," I said, "but, you see, the tables do not have any labels. I didn't know. But tomorrow, I will find out where New York sits here, and then I will go to New York." So I continued to eat, and he continues— [*laughter*]

CHISHOLM: "You're sitting at the Georgia delegation table." And I said, "I says if you don't—" [*laughter*]

CHISHOLM: —"if you don't move from here, I will so and so and so." But then I began to feel sorry for him, because he was hungry, and I decided to use a different psychological approach.

I said, "You're hungry, aren't you?" And it's the first time he gave me a smile because I was nice to him. He said, "Sure, I'm hungry." I said, "I know what your problem is. Your problem is you cannot sit at this table because a black person is seated at the table. Isn't that right?" He said, "Yeah." [*laughter*]

CHISHOLM: I said, "I am going to help you. You see that table over there?" There's a table diagonally across from the table where I was sitting, and there's nobody at it.

I said, "Look, you go over and you sit at that table, you order your lunch, and if anybody bothers you, you tell 'em to see Shirley Chisholm."

And I thought this would embarrass him, but it did not. This was just the funniest thing to me. It did not embarrass him. He went right over to the table and he sat— [*laughter*]

CHISHOLM: And he sat down!

COSBY: That just proves how ludicrous all this is, doesn't it?

CHISHOLM: It's ridiculous.

Then, then this other one—and this almost brought the house down. There was a gentleman that sat on the aisle seat, on the aisle, on the House floor. My office was on the other side of the building, so when I would come to the floor, he could see me coming through because my office was on that side of the building, upstairs, and he could see me coming down, because where I was going to sit was right behind him.

And every day I would come down and come through, and he would cough so badly. So one day I said to Brock Adams, who was the representative from the State of Washington, I said, "Why don't somebody do something for that poor man. He sounds like he has TB. There's something wrong with him." And he said, "Shirley, I was waiting for you." He said, "I want to tell you something. You got to do something."

I said, "What?" He said, "Every time he sees you coming down and coming through, he starts coughing, and then when you come by his seat, he gets his handkerchief out, he spits in the handkerchief, in your face." This was his way of greeting me in the United States House of Representatives.

I said, "He does, Brock?" I said, "I thought—" He said, "Uh-uh. What are you going to do about it?"

I said, "Watch me tomorrow."

I had a sweater suit, and the jacket, the jacket of the sweater had big pockets. And I went out and I bought, I purchased, a male handkerchief and I put it in the pocket, and the next day, when I came in, sure enough, he started to cough. I said, "Uh-huh. Baby, I'm going to fix you today."

So, just as I came in, he was walking by the seat; by then I had it synchronized as to when he would pull the handkerchief out to meet my face and then spit in the handkerchief.

I said, "Yes, sir." That day, pulled a handkerchief out just in time to spit in it and put it, throw it, in his face, and I said to him, "Beat you to it today." [*laughter*]

CHISHOLM: From that day, he never coughed anymore.

COSBY: I bet he didn't! There is that persistence. Yes. Not putting up with nonsense.

CHISHOLM: Yes, that's right. That's right. And the men—I'll never forget—the men upstairs in the balcony, there was the newspapermen, and they saw this from upstairs in the balcony as I was coming in, and they almost toppled over the top. They roared, and the speaker had to put the— "There'll be order in this House."

COSBY: But, you know, it sounds like you also had allies.

CHISHOLM: Oh, yes.

COSBY: Because people were roaring, for example.

CHISHOLM: Oh, yeah, and another thing. The House would be so boring, at times, that they'd do anything, you know, to have some—"Shirley, give it to him, give to him, give it to him." [*fists clapping*] You know. [*laughter*]

COSBY: Boy, that sounds like a very interesting beginning for you.

CHISHOLM: Uh-huh, uh-huh.

COSBY: What social and political issues were your priorities to fight for while you served in Congress, especially in the beginning of your career in Congress?

CHISHOLM: It's the same old priority that we have today.

COSBY: Yes.

CHISHOLM: Housing. Employment. Health. The same priorities follow black people in these United States time after time after time.

COSBY: So your priorities were the same issues that people are still fighting for today.

CHISHOLM: Yes, the same issues. It's strange that they don't change.

COSBY: That is strange, isn't it?

CHISHOLM: Yes, it's strange that they don't change. Uh-huh.

COSBY: Now, even including a woman's right to choose, the abortion issue, educational issues, housing, so forth—people who are conscientious are still fighting for the same—

CHISHOLM: Still fighting for the same thing.

COSBY: What do you think about this current political climate? Do you think that there will be more obstacles that will be set up to—so that people cannot penetrate and get those particular rights?

CHISHOLM: Well, it's being done very subtly in many instances, but our country has definitely moved to the right, there's no question about it, and so you find a kind of—what should I say? There's a cutback on the kind of funding that is so necessary to help lower-class and middle-class people to at least gain some opportunities.

So in some instances it's worse than it used to be.

COSBY: Do you think, Ms. Chisholm, that it's the country, or, or do you think it's really the politicians and those who finance them?

CHISHOLM: It's the politicians.

COSBY: The politicians.

CHISHOLM: Oh, yes, the politicians. There's no question about it.

COSBY: And of course we have the media to do the spin, and the people might be led to support the politicians.

CHISHOLM: That's right.

COSBY: Do you think that's true?

CHISHOLM: That's right. Very true.

COSBY: I see. Now after you went into Congress, were you at the National Black Political Convention in 1972?

CHISHOLM: You mean at Gary?

COSBY: Yes, in Gary, Indiana.

CHISHOLM: No.

COSBY: No, you weren't. I see. Do you think that that particular gathering was significant?

CHISHOLM: No. I would have to say it was very significant because they were attempting to run a black person for the presidency of the United States, but they got into so many quarrels and fights. And of course I was not invited, nor would I be invited, because I had already put my hat in the ring to make a bid for the presidency.

COSBY: Despite it all.

CHISHOLM: Despite it all.

COSBY: What made you decide to do this, to run for president of the United States?

CHISHOLM: What made me decide was that I felt that the time had come, when a black person, or a female person, could and should be president of these United States of America, not only white males. And I decided somebody had to get it started.

COSBY: Were you the first black?

CHISHOLM: Yes, yes.

COSBY: Not only the first black woman, but the first black to run for president of the United States.

CHISHOLM: That's right. And what I did, I felt that just about four years before, I had gone to the Congress as the first black woman to be elected to the Congress. And I had gone on a number of speaking engagements through the country, and there was a fantastic development for me as an individual, and people were encouraging me. "Ms. Chisholm, you should run. You should run because you're a woman. We never had a woman president. You're black. We never had a black person for president. You speak Spanish. You have a knowledge of the issues. Run."

And that's what motivated me—

COSBY: Just spurred you on.

CHISHOLM: Yes, spurred me on. But I knew I would be in trouble, because the moment that the announcement was

made that I was going to make a bid for the presidency, all
hell broke loose. All hell broke loose, from black men, white
men, Puerto Rican men. Hell broke loose.

COSBY: Yes.

CHISHOLM: See, and I kind of expected it. I expected it.

COSBY: I do remember that period, too, when you announced
your candidacy.

CHISHOLM: Yes.

COSBY: And how people were mumbling about this woman
running—

CHISHOLM: Yes. "This woman."

COSBY: How dare she do this?

CHISHOLM: Yes, yes. That's right.

COSBY: And there you were.

CHISHOLM: Uh-huh.

COSBY: Do you think that you are publicly acknowledged for
paving the way for women who have run for political offices
and have won?

CHISHOLM: I think I'm publicly acknowledged, to a degree.

COSBY: To a degree?

CHISHOLM: Yes, to a degree. Uh-huh.

But one thing about it is that—sometimes I've caused this myself. I—believe it or not, you might not really want to accept this—that I'm a very reserved person, really. I am not a person that goes in for a lot of hullabaloo and everything, unless I'm fighting for a cause.

And there are many, many things that have been said to me and asked of me that I would not do, because I really don't like a lot of hullabaloo. So I would not say that it was due to people. Partially, it's due to me also.

COSBY: No. I believe that. I mean, I have seen some people who are public people who can be very still in the midst of being surrounded by a lot of people.

CHISHOLM: Yes, correct.

COSBY: I suppose that is what you're talking about, that you really find that quiet center, despite the fact that you are surrounded by many, but you need your quiet time so that you can be regenerated for the public? Is that what you mean?

CHISHOLM: Yes, that's right. Definitely.

COSBY: Yes. Because during that time, when you ran for, for the president, it must have been absolutely chaotic.

CHISHOLM: Oh, it was!

COSBY: And the media—did you think that the media treated you properly overall?

CHISHOLM: No. They did not treat me properly at all, particularly in the South. But the one thing in the South that was very strange was George Wallace.

COSBY: Oh, yes.

CHISHOLM: George Wallace, for some strange, unknown reason, he liked me, and when we were running in the Floridian primary, John Lindsay, who was the mayor of New York, begged me to pull back because I was beating him in Florida, and I would not pull back. I said, "No, this is my time."

COSBY: Oh, that is such a surprise that you would not do that. [*laughter*]

CHISHOLM: I would not. George Wallace came down to Florida, and he went all over Florida and he, he said to the people, "If you all can't vote for me, don't vote for those oval-headed lynchers. Vote for Shirley Chisholm." And that crashed my votes, because they thought I was in league with him to get votes.

COSBY: Oh.

CHISHOLM: That's what killed me in Florida. You see? Because he came out for me, if people couldn't vote for him. So they said, well, I guess Shirley Chisholm made some kind of agreement with George Wallace—

COSBY: Behind the scenes.

CHISHOLM: Yes, that's right.

COSBY: And then, of course, when he was shot you visited him, and I understand there—

CHISHOLM: Oh, when I visited him, and he was shot, I almost lost my seat. I went to the hospital to visit him, and all of us who were running for president at that time—Jackson and Wilbur Mills and John Lindsay—there were thirteen of us who were out there in the race in 1972. And I went to see him. Oh, my gosh! I knew that I was going to be thrown out of office.

The people in my district came down on me like anything, and I had two big public forums, and I said this is not the way we do it. And I had to lecture to them and let them know that I wouldn't want this to happen to anybody. So I kind of brought them along, but that was one time that I almost lost my seat, even though I was still holding, because I went to visit George Wallace.

And when I went to visit George Wallace, he was in the bed—I'll never forget this—all the tubes were coming through his nostrils, his throat, and he was lying in the bed, and he was propped up, and I come in through the door, and he says, "Shirley Chisholm, what you doing here? You shouldn't be here." I said, "I'm here because you are ill, and you are ill for a good reason. God guides us."

And he, he looked up. I couldn't stay long because he was very ill, and the doctors told me, "Congresswoman, you have to leave him." And he held on to my hand so tightly, he didn't want me to go.

COSBY: Because that was the beginning of his transition, wasn't it?

CHISHOLM: Yes, yes.

COSBY: After he was shot.

CHISHOLM: Yes. And I tell you it—that was, that was one of the moments in my life, my district almost ripped me apart.

COSBY: What did you do, Ms. Chisholm to, to correct that?

CHISHOLM: I had to lecture a—I don't have it now—but I have a way of speaking, I have a way of being able to draw people to me, and I use it. It was my ability to have an influence on people by the way I speak and the way I dress, and what have you. And that's what helped.

COSBY: I see.

CHISHOLM: If not, I would have been out. I would have been out of office.

COSBY: I see.

CHISHOLM: Uh-huh.

COSBY: So you're, you're saying that your speaking skills and, and your people skills— you used those two skills to turn this negativity around.

CHISHOLM: Correct.

COSBY: Because, I suppose, that the media had also played a part in this to make you appear to be undesirable.

CHISHOLM: Yes, that's right.

COSBY: And you were already this black woman running for president. So you were dealing with many negative issues there.

CHISHOLM: Uh-huh.

COSBY: Many of the nation's black political leadership, including some in your own Congressional Black Caucus, did not support you.

CHISHOLM: Uh-huh.

COSBY: Why? [*laughter*]

CHISHOLM: They didn't support me because, first of all, the seat belongs to a man; belongs to a male, period, white male, Puerto Rican male. Belongs to a male. No women have any right—or should have any right running for the presidency of the United States.

COSBY: Well, certainly a white male for president.

CHISHOLM: That's right. And then, secondly, these men wanted to put forth a black male for president, and I got in the way, and the thing about it, as you said, I'm a very tenacious person. I held on; I wouldn't give up. I wouldn't step back. And that was it.

COSBY: And what was your reaction to this, this negative attitude from the men within the Black Caucus, or maybe other people as well?

CHISHOLM: I didn't pay them any mind. I looked neither to the South nor to the North, to the West nor to the East. And whatever I do, even today, I look only to God and my conscience for approval, not man. That's my motto. You go crazy if you look to man. [*laughter*]

COSBY: What was your presidential platform?

CHISHOLM: My platform was things that I was talking to you earlier about. Education. Better housing. Paying attention to our health problems, the health problems, that was always the same things.

COSBY: Always the same issues.

CHISHOLM: Always the same.

COSBY: Welfare, too, I suppose.

CHISHOLM: Yes, yes, yes.

COSBY: Wow! It is awful, isn't it?

CHISHOLM: Yes.

COSBY: However, there were some black men who supported you.

CHISHOLM: Oh, yes. Uh-huh.

COSBY: I understand that Ron Dellums and Parren Mitchell—

CHISHOLM: Uh-huh.

COSBY: At least, you know, there were some very conscientious men in this group.

CHISHOLM: Yes. There, there were some, and these conscientious men, Ron Dellums and Parren Mitchell, they were trying to talk to their brothers and say give her a chance, she has ability, she has talent. Shirley's no dummy. And they, they so much as told them, "Get lost."

COSBY: But how wonderful that they did that despite the fact that most of their peers did not.

CHISHOLM: Yes, that's right.

COSBY: Oh, hooray to them. What went through your mind as your name went into the nomination at the 1972 Democratic National Convention? [*laughter*]

COSBY: Just when you heard your name?

CHISHOLM: Well, you know, I was embarrassed. You know, I don't know what it was. But George Wallace, his delegates, they jumped outta their seats and strumming, "Go Shirley, go." You know, I couldn't understand this, that southerners, particularly from the State of Alabama, because the State of the Alabama was seated right down front at the convention center, and they almost went wild—and, and all the people from New York and Pennsylvania, they were looking like, "What's going on here?" Shirley's supporting them? You know, I couldn't control it.

For some reason—I would like to understand this, why the State of Alabama, led by George Wallace at that time, had good feelings, good vibes about me. It's very strange.

COSBY: That is.

CHISHOLM: Yeah, very strange.

COSBY: You don't think it was a setup in any way, do you?

CHISHOLM: No, no.

COSBY: To dilute your power?

CHISHOLM: I don't think so. I don't know what it was, but they really—

COSBY: That must have been quite a sight to see, these delegates from Alabama—

CHISHOLM: I wanted to tell them, "Sit down, sit down." You know what I mean? [*laughter*]

COSBY: Now George McGovern of course was the ultimate nominee for the Democrat Party against Nixon.

CHISHOLM: Uh-huh.

COSBY: Besides yourself, who would you have favored to be the nominee? Or what would you consider to be a winning ticket, besides yourself, at that time?

CHISHOLM: I thought that Humphrey should be on the ticket, should be the person.

COSBY: With McGovern you mean?

CHISHOLM: Yes.

COSBY: I see. And why?

CHISHOLM: Well, Humphrey, in terms of his political life, had always taken very strong and firm positions on the issues that affected poor people and people from the middle class.

COSBY: Because he had a solid civil rights record.

CHISHOLM: Yes, that's right.

COSBY: What about George McGovern?

CHISHOLM: I never did care that much for George McGovern. I thought that George McGovern was just an opportunist, at that time.

COSBY: Yes. But why do you think he lost to Nixon?

CHISHOLM: 'Cause he didn't have support. He didn't have support because the only state that he carried in the union, which is very embarrassing, was Massachusetts.

COSBY: Really?

CHISHOLM: Yes. He didn't carry any state at the convention but Massachusetts.

COSBY: That's just amazing.

CHISHOLM: Yes, yes. Massachusetts was the only state that, that really backed him. And I think he was a little bit—you know, if you're going into politics, you have to show by your behavior and your actions that you care for people, that you like people, and he was somewhat—he was a little bit stuffy. He, he couldn't—

COSBY: A little distant.

CHISHOLM: Yeah, a little distant. He couldn't consort with people easily. It was very noticeable.

COSBY: I see.

CHISHOLM: I think that did not help him.

COSBY: So the personality was a problem?

CHISHOLM: Yes, yes, that's right. That's right.

COSBY: What was the greatest lesson you learned about America and its political system?

CHISHOLM: The greatest lesson I learned about America is that America must not feel so terribly superior to everybody else in the world.

COSBY: Do you feel that is very evident now?

CHISHOLM: Now, even today, America feels that she knows

everything, and that she has a right, a God-given right, to tell people how to live, how to do whatever. I have very deep feelings about that. America suffers from a superiority complex of the worst kind.

COSBY: And what do you think will be the ramifications from that attitude?

CHISHOLM: I think we're going to get ourselves in the position of more and more people disliking us, because we act so arrogant. We always want to tell everybody else what to do.

COSBY: Do you think that America's populace is aware of this?

CHISHOLM: No. I don't think they're aware of it.

COSBY: They're not aware of the architects of all of this arrogance and colonialism?

CHISHOLM: They follow the politicians, what the politicians tell them, you see. Americans are very, very gullible.

COSBY: Ms. Chisholm, why do you think Americans are so gullible? I'm talking about the populace now. Why do they want to follow and not question, do you think? Not be critical thinkers.

CHISHOLM: Critical thinkers?

COSBY: Yes. [*laughter*]

COSBY: Is there any such thing? [*laughter*]

CHISHOLM: Americans—I think the largest thing—I wouldn't say that we're not smart. We just don't have time to think. Our lives are so complicated and so complex; we have so many things to do in America. There's no other country in the world where people are involved in so many different things, and responsible for so many . . .

And then also I think there's a little bit of laziness in terms of using your brainpower. I really do.

COSBY: Of course we're talking about how the American populace, so many people are gullible.

CHISHOLM: Uh-huh.

COSBY: Do you think it has anything to do with fear? Because most people in America, I assume, are middle income—

CHISHOLM: Yes, they are.

COSBY: And middle-income people are in debt.

CHISHOLM: Uh-huh.

COSBY: I mean, they, they have to pay mortgages, they have to pay car notes.

CHISHOLM: Uh-huh.

COSBY: Most of the things that they own, they had to borrow from the bank to get.

CHISHOLM: Uh-huh.

COSBY: So there has to be a fear, I think, about losing one's job and then losing everything that one has—

CHISHOLM: Uh-huh.

COSBY: —that has not been paid for yet. Do you think that might be one factor for the populace being so gullible?

CHISHOLM: I think one of the basic factors is the fact that the American people don't have the time to think of anything else. There's so many problems. There's no other country in the world in which citizens have so many problems and so many things to think about.

COSBY: So the time is spent working to pay for everything perhaps.

CHISHOLM: Yes, yes. They don't—it's a strange thing, but they just don't have time to—

How many Americans are really interested in politics? They only become quite interested when it's time to, for, the candidates to run for office and they have to make selections. But all during the course of the year they don't think about—

COSBY: They're not interested.

CHISHOLM: They're not interested. You know, they're really not interested.

COSBY: Probably because they don't know how important it is to be—

CHISHOLM: That's right. They don't realize.

COSBY: If they really knew what the politicians were doing, that affects all of our lives, maybe there would be more interest.

CHISHOLM: Uh-huh, uh-huh.

COSBY: But I have found that so many people are afraid to face the truth; it's a little unsettling, because so many of us like to feel comfortable.

CHISHOLM: That's right.

COSBY: We don't want to know what the truth is because it might be horrifying.

CHISHOLM: That's right.

COSBY: So do you think that that is one of the problems in terms of people not becoming interested in what the politicians are doing?

CHISHOLM: I think so. They just want to sit back, just take care of the things that they have to take care of, things that affect their daily lives, and don't bother me with all these other things. You know?

COSBY: Yes, yes. And then of course most of the politicians are men, and we have a tendency to look at men as gods.

CHISHOLM: Yes.

COSBY: Was it difficult to return to Congress after your campaign for president?

CHISHOLM: No, it was not difficult.

COSBY: No?

CHISHOLM: I became even more popular. I became more popular, you know.

COSBY: More popular?

CHISHOLM: Yeah, more popular.

COSBY: Was there any noticeable change in the way your colleagues treated you in Congress?

CHISHOLM: Oh, yes. They treated me—it was strange. They didn't realize I was "so smart," in quotes. They—the men—some of them approached me, and said, "You got a brain." I said, "I've always had a brain." [*laughter*]

CHISHOLM: You know—they belittle women so badly. [*laughter*]

COSBY: Do you think that that is still a problem?

CHISHOLM: Oh, no, it's gone. No. Because the women that we have in Congress now, we have forty-three women in Congress.

COSBY: Yes.

CHISHOLM: They give 'em the business!

COSBY: They do.

CHISHOLM: Oh, yes. They give 'em the business. I wouldn't be surprised, another, let's say another ten years from now, if we don't have half and half.

COSBY: Yes.

CHISHOLM: I will not be surprised.

COSBY: Let's hope so.

CHISHOLM: More and more women are getting the guts to run.

COSBY: What about for the presidency?

CHISHOLM: Oh, a woman is going to be president.

COSBY: Within the next ten years, maybe?

CHISHOLM: Next twenty-five years.

COSBY: Twenty-five years.

CHISHOLM: Yes, yes. A woman's going to be president.

COSBY: Yes. Do you think it will be a woman of color?

CHISHOLM: No. I believe that before a woman can become president of this country, a woman has to be vice president, first of all, so that we will get used to the idea of a woman ascending to high office. That's what I believe.

COSBY: I see.

CHISHOLM: Yeah.

COSBY: Fantastic.

In 1982, you decided not to seek another term in Congress. Why did you make that decision?

CHISHOLM: Reagan. [*laughter*]

COSBY: Tell us about Reagan.

CHISHOLM: Many of the programs, and many of the things

that I'd been interested in, I saw how they deteriorated. I saw how many things were pushed back on the back burner, and many of the things that I had been involved in were no longer a part of his overall domestic programs. It was just too much. I said I didn't want to go through it anymore.

COSBY: That was it.

CHISHOLM: That was it. I had enough. Yes, that was it.

COSBY: What do you consider to be your greatest legislative victory?

CHISHOLM: The income for domestics in this country. Domestic workers. Every year we had the increase in income, domestic workers never, never fit into the scale of things.

COSBY: Are you talking about minimum wage?

CHISHOLM: No. Just in general.

COSBY: In general.

CHISHOLM: In general. Domestics were just—they were treated almost like animals.

COSBY: Yes. What about benefits?

CHISHOLM: And the title program, the Title 2, the Title 1 program of the Education Act.

COSBY: Oh.

CHISHOLM: Yes. Title—is it Title . . .? I can't remember the title, whether it's Title 2 or Title 1. And then Title 9.

COSBY: Yes.

CHISHOLM: I am very proud of the fact that Title 9, I had a very, very big part in that, because of the fact that for the first time, women in this country, and women on the college campuses, could compete for athletic scholarships.

COSBY: Oh.

CHISHOLM: Women could never get athletic scholarships.

COSBY: Isn't that something!

CHISHOLM: Yes. Women could never get athletic scholarships, and I fought for that, and today women—

COSBY: Oh, all over the place.

CHISHOLM: Yeah, yeah, all over the place. Yeah. Very proud of that. [*laughter*]

CHISHOLM: Yes. I'm proud of that.

COSBY: You were a professor at Mount Holyoke College.

CHISHOLM: Yes. I was.

COSBY: From 1983 to 1987. What did you teach, and was the teaching as satisfactory as politics?

CHISHOLM: Oh, I taught politics. I taught women in politics and—I guess it was women in politics and the growth of the women's movement in this country.

COSBY: I bet you had full classes.

CHISHOLM: Oh, my gosh! They were overcrowded; classes were overcrowded.

COSBY: And that's such a beautiful campus, too.

CHISHOLM: Yes, yes. I had a wonderful experience there. I had a very wonderful experience there, but I realized that many of the women whom I taught, they knew absolutely nothing about the importance, in this country, with respect to the development of women in the field of politics.

They didn't know anything, you know. It was a revelation to me, how little we knew about ourselves. Women.

COSBY: Even at a women's institution like Mount Holyoke.

CHISHOLM: Yes.

COSBY: What about when you went to Spelman? I understand you were a visiting professor there.

CHISHOLM: The same thing.

COSBY: The same thing at Spelman?

CHISHOLM: The same thing, yes.

COSBY: Why do you think that's so?

CHISHOLM: Look, your universities, your professional staff is composed mainly of men, and they just don't stress the importance of women. They just don't—I don't think they do it purposely. I think it never enters their mind, that women have made a fantastic contribution to this country. They just never think of it.

COSBY: What about the women professors, though?

CHISHOLM: They're so few and far between.

COSBY: Really?

CHISHOLM: Yes. There's so few in there, far between, and the women I find, also, some of them are very much afraid of male professors. They don't want to—

COSBY: Once again that godlike image.

CHISHOLM: Yeah, yes, yes. It's something that I have not been able to get used to.

COSBY: I guess not.

CHISHOLM: I guess I'm so outspoken and I, I am so free.

COSBY: Also, I find it so interesting, Ms. Chisholm, to go back to your Caribbean background, because in my mind, I always thought that these different Caribbean cultures were very male oriented.

CHISHOLM: Oh, yes!

COSBY: But still, you, you obviously felt that you were equal to men in terms of intelligence and whatever, you know, pursuing your goals and so forth. I still would like to know, is it because of your grandmother? Is it because these women said, "No, Ms. Chisholm, Shirley, you are equal to." Is that—

CHISHOLM: It's my grandmother.

COSBY: Your grandmother said it.

CHISHOLM: My grandmother had an impact—

COSBY: It was a mantra.

CHISHOLM: Yes. My grandmother had such an impact on my life, that had she not had this impact on me, I don't think I would have moved out in this country like I did. I really believe that.

COSBY: Oh, my goodness; it was a powerful impact.

CHISHOLM: Yes, it was. It was.

COSBY: Because you definitely have gone against the odds. In many ways.

CHISHOLM: Yes.

COSBY: How would you describe yourself? [*laughter*]

CHISHOLM: I would describe myself as—I'll have to use adjectives, huh? [*laughter*]

COSBY: Okay. Whatever.

CHISHOLM: I would describe myself as being friendly, a very extroverted personality, a lover of people, a person who smiles, who laughs a great deal, a person with a kind of sense of humor. Imitator of people. I like to imitate and copy people. [*laughter*]

CHISHOLM: And a very tenacious person, a very determined person, and a person who does not believe in following other people for the sake of following them. Going on the dictates of my mind and my conscience.

COSBY: Very good. And what is your definition of leadership? And, definitely, you have been a leader.

CHISHOLM: A leader has to know that he knows, and he has to be—

COSBY: Or she.

CHISHOLM: Yeah, he or she. He has to be able to withstand the insults and the kind of things that are thrown in your direction, and you have to really have a spirit and a mind, which dictates only to you, and to know within yourself that what you are doing is the right thing to do, because that's what you feel. And you should not look to anybody at all for approval of what you are about.

And a leader has to learn to stand at the head of the flock and beckon them to follow.

COSBY: And what do you think has been the major misperception of you?

CHISHOLM: Oh. I think I would have to say that people, many people felt that I've rarely been too outspoken, that I should hold back a bit. That's one of the things I know. That you're too outspoken. Don't always speak out on everything that you feel. I can't help it. I'm too outspoken, is what they've told me.

COSBY: But, of course, you don't think you are too outspoken.

CHISHOLM: No. I don't.

COSBY: No, of course not. What do you consider to be your greatest achievement?

CHISHOLM: My greatest achievement, believe it or not, is that I had the audacity and the nerve to make a bid for the presidency of the United States of America. I really think that's my greatest achievement.

COSBY: What is your strongest regret?

CHISHOLM: You know, to tell you the truth, I don't really regret anything that I've done. I really don't.

COSBY: Very good.

CHISHOLM: Uh-huh.

COSBY: What advice would you want to give to young blacks?

CHISHOLM: Get a good education, follow your mind, follow the dictates of your conscience, do what you think and feel has to be done in order for you to achieve, and you'll be able to succeed. I really believe that.

COSBY: Do you think that young blacks feel hopeful?

CHISHOLM: No. I don't.

COSBY: Do you think that that is self-defeating, if you're hopeless?

CHISHOLM: Yes, yes. Yes.

COSBY: So what, what can be done to make young people see that they can be hopeful?

CHISHOLM: All you can do, you can constantly lecture to them, and constantly answer their queries and their, their questions about things. But so much of it has to do with the kind of environment in which they're reared.

COSBY: Yes. Then of course young people are bombarded with negative images, too.

CHISHOLM: Oh, yes. Yes.

COSBY: From different forms of media.

CHISHOLM: That's right.

COSBY: So that those repetitive messages, perhaps, are making them feel hopeless, or defining them—that they believe these definitions.

CHISHOLM: Yes.

COSBY: What can be done, do you think? What can be done to counter these repetitive negative messages and images?

CHISHOLM: I still say that basically, you always have to go back to the environment in which they're being reared. You always have to go back to that.

I know of young people—I had to get a few of them straightened out a few weeks ago—don't give me that answer, don't tell me that. They didn't want to get high marks in their class because it means that they think they're "it." They, they just want to be mediocre individuals.

And I told them, there's too much mediocrity in this country. Too much.

COSBY: Yes.

CHISHOLM: You've got to excel because excellence reaps rewards.

COSBY: And I daresay that those of us who have been fortunate enough to be exposed to people who are in charge, we see more mediocrity the closer we get to the people who are in charge. Would you agree with that? [*laughter*]

CHISHOLM: Oh, gosh! Yes. Yes.

COSBY: Are you optimistic about America's racial future?

CHISHOLM: No.

COSBY: Why is that?

CHISHOLM: If our very basic Constitution had phrases in it that had to do with slavery, and if we go back to the birth of this country, and the growth of this country, and if we go back to laws and rules and regulations of the states, I can't be optimistic. I try to be, but I can't. I can't be optimistic.

COSBY: And the, the fact that people have fought so hard for the amendments to the Constitution, to make the Constitution what it's supposed to be, that, too, I guess—

CHISHOLM: I can't be optimistic. I've tried to look at it in a way that I don't see a lot of loopholes or what have you; but I find that I can't. I'm not very optimistic about my country, and I love my country. I love my country but I can't be too optimistic about it.

COSBY: What do you think that we'll do if someone like you, Ms. Chisholm, is not optimistic; how can we make young people more persistent, like you were persistent, to make, to create the changes, to galvanize people so that they will become critical thinkers and be activists? If there's a lack of optimism, I mean, what is the, the component to make you—

CHISHOLM: But, you see, what I always say, I always go back, constantly, to the environment in which they are being reared. You have to go back to how they're being reared. What is being discussed with them at home? What is being said to them when they go out? It goes right back to the home.

COSBY: It does.

CHISHOLM: If you don't have a good home background, forget it.

COSBY: And then there are so many changes that need to be done in the home—

CHISHOLM: You open that door, you open that door and the young people go off. You only pray that they come back the way you sent them out.

COSBY: Yes.

CHISHOLM: It's very hard.

COSBY: Ms. Chisholm, how do you want history to remember you?

CHISHOLM: I want history to remember me, not that I was the first black woman to be elected to the Congress, not as the first black woman to have made a bid for the presidency of the United States, but as a black woman who lived in the twentieth century and who dared to be herself. I want to be remembered as a catalyst for change in America.

COSBY: Thank you, Ms. Chisholm.

SHIRLEY CHISHOLM was born to Caribbean immigrants in Brooklyn, New York. She ran for Congress in the newly drawn Twelfth District of New York in 1968 and became the first-ever black woman to serve in Congress after an upset, grassroots-powered victory. She went on to run for president in 1972. While in Congress, she was instrumental in creating the National School Lunch Program, expanding the food stamp program, and establishing the Special Supplemental Nutrition Program for Women, Infants, and Children. She passed away on January 1, 2005.

BARBARA LEE has served as U.S. Representative for California's 13th congressional district since 1998. Before she started her own political career, she worked on Shirley Chisholm's 1972 campaign for president and served as a delegate for Rep. Chisholm at the 1972 Democratic National Convention in Miami, FL.

SUSAN BROWNMILLER is an American feminist journalist, author, and activist, best known for her 1975 book *Against Our Will: Men, Women, and Rape.*

MIRIAM ROSEN was a producer at Pacifica Radio.

LARRY KEETER is professor emeritus in the Department of Sociology and Anthropology in the College of Arts and Sciences at Appalachian State University. Keeter began teaching at Appalachian State in 1971 and served as mayor of Boone, North Carolina, from 1985 to 1989.

CAMILLE COSBY is a theatrical and television producer. She cofounded the National Visionary Leadership Project with Renee Poussaint in 2001.

THE LAST INTERVIEW SERIES

RUTH BADER GINSBURG : THE LAST INTERVIEW AND OTHER CONVERSATIONS

"No one ever expected me to go to law school. I was supposed to be a high school teacher, or how else could I earn a living?"

$17.99 / $22.99 CAN
978-1-61219-919-1
ebook: 978-1-61219-920-7

MARILYN MONROE: THE LAST INTERVIEW AND OTHER CONVERSATIONS

"I'm so many people. They shock me sometimes. I wish I was just me!"

$16.99 / $21.99 CAN
978-1-61219-877-4
ebook: 978-1-61219-878-1

FRIDA KAHLO: THE LAST INTERVIEW AND OTHER CONVERSATIONS

"The only thing I know is that I paint because I need to, and I paint always whatever passes through my head, without any other consideration."

$16.99 / $21.99 CAN
978-1-61219-875-0
ebook: 978-1-61219-876-7

THE LAST INTERVIEW SERIES

TONI MORRISON: THE LAST INTERVIEW AND OTHER CONVERSATIONS

"Knowledge is what's important, you know? Not the erasure, but the confrontation of it."

$16.99 / 21.99 CAN
978-1-61219-873-6
ebook: 978-1-61219-874-3

GRAHAM GREENE: THE LAST INTERVIEW AND OTHER CONVERSATIONS

"I think to exclude politics from a novel is to exclude a whole aspect of life."

$16.99 / 21.99 CAN
978-1-61219-814-9
ebook: 978-1-61219-815-6

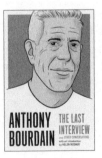

ANTHONY BOURDAIN: THE LAST INTERVIEW AND OTHER CONVERSATIONS

"We should feed our enemies Chicken McNuggets."

$16.99 / $21.99 CAN
978-1-61219-824-8
ebook: 978-1-61219-825-5

THE LAST INTERVIEW SERIES

URSULA K. LE GUIN: THE LAST INTERVIEW AND OTHER CONVERSATIONS

"Resistance and change often begin in art.
Very often in our art, the art of words."

$16.99 / $21.99 CAN
978-1-61219-779-1
ebook: 978-1-61219-780-7

PRINCE: THE LAST INTERVIEW AND OTHER CONVERSATIONS

"That's what you want. Transcendence.
When that happens—oh, boy."

$16.99 / $22.99 CAN
978-1-61219-745-6
ebook: 978-1-61219-746-3

JULIA CHILD: THE LAST INTERVIEW AND OTHER CONVERSATIONS

"I'm not a chef, I'm a teacher and a cook."

$16.99 / $22.99 CAN
978-1-61219-733-3
ebook: 978-1-61219-734-0

THE LAST INTERVIEW SERIES

KURT VONNEGUT: THE LAST INTERVIEW

"I think it can be tremendously refreshing if a creator of literature has something on his mind other than the history of literature so far. Literature should not disappear up its own asshole, so to speak."

$15.95 / $17.95 CAN
978-1-61219-090-7
ebook: 978-1-61219-091-4

JACQUES DERRIDA: THE LAST INTERVIEW
LEARNING TO LIVE FINALLY

"I am at war with myself, it's true, you couldn't possibly know to what extent... I say contradictory things that are, we might say, in real tension; they are what construct me, make me live, and will make me die."

translated by PASCAL-ANNE BRAULT and MICHAEL NAAS

$15.95 / $17.95 CAN
978-1-61219-094-5
ebook: 978-1-61219-032-7

ROBERTO BOLAÑO: THE LAST INTERVIEW

"Posthumous: It sounds like the name of a Roman gladiator, an unconquered gladiator. At least that's what poor Posthumous would like to believe. It gives him courage."

translated by SYBIL PEREZ and others

$15.95 / $17.95 CAN
978-1-61219-095-2
ebook: 978-1-61219-033-4

THE LAST INTERVIEW SERIES

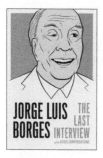

JORGE LUIS BORGES: THE LAST INTERVIEW

"Believe me: the benefits of blindness have been greatly exaggerated. If I could see, I would never leave the house, I'd stay indoors reading the many books that surround me."

translated by KIT MAUDE

$15.95 / $15.95 CAN
978-1-61219-204-8
ebook: 978-1-61219-205-5

HANNAH ARENDT: THE LAST INTERVIEW

"There are no dangerous thoughts for the simple reason that thinking itself is such a dangerous enterprise."

$15.95 / $15.95 CAN
978-1-61219-311-3
ebook: 978-1-61219-312-0

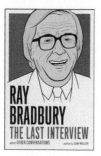

RAY BRADBURY: THE LAST INTERVIEW

"You don't have to destroy books to destroy a culture. Just get people to stop reading them."

$15.95 / $15.95 CAN
978-1-61219-421-9
ebook: 978-1-61219-422-6

THE LAST INTERVIEW SERIES

KURT VONNEGUT: THE LAST INTERVIEW

"I think it can be tremendously refreshing if a creator of literature has something on his mind other than the history of literature so far. Literature should not disappear up its own asshole, so to speak."

$15.95 / $17.95 CAN
978-1-61219-090-7
ebook: 978-1-61219-091-4

JACQUES DERRIDA: THE LAST INTERVIEW
LEARNING TO LIVE FINALLY

"I am at war with myself, it's true, you couldn't possibly know to what extent... I say contradictory things that are, we might say, in real tension; they are what construct me, make me live, and will make me die."

translated by PASCAL-ANNE BRAULT and MICHAEL NAAS

$15.95 / $17.95 CAN
978-1-61219-094-5
ebook: 978-1-61219-032-7

ROBERTO BOLAÑO: THE LAST INTERVIEW

"Posthumous: It sounds like the name of a Roman gladiator, an unconquered gladiator. At least that's what poor Posthumous would like to believe. It gives him courage."

translated by SYBIL PEREZ and others

$15.95 / $17.95 CAN
978-1-61219-095-2
ebook: 978-1-61219-033-4

THE LAST INTERVIEW SERIES

JORGE LUIS BORGES: THE LAST INTERVIEW

"Believe me: the benefits of blindness have been greatly exaggerated. If I could see, I would never leave the house, I'd stay indoors reading the many books that surround me."

translated by KIT MAUDE

$15.95 / $15.95 CAN
978-1-61219-204-8
ebook: 978-1-61219-205-5

HANNAH ARENDT: THE LAST INTERVIEW

"There are no dangerous thoughts for the simple reason that thinking itself is such a dangerous enterprise."

$15.95 / $15.95 CAN
978-1-61219-311-3
ebook: 978-1-61219-312-0

RAY BRADBURY: THE LAST INTERVIEW

"You don't have to destroy books to destroy a culture. Just get people to stop reading them."

$15.95 / $15.95 CAN
978-1-61219-421-9
ebook: 978-1-61219-422-6

JANE JACOBS: THE LAST INTERVIEW

"I would like it to be understood that all our human economic achievements have been done by ordinary people, not by exceptionally educated people, or by elites, or by supernatural forces."

$15.95 / $20.95 CAN
978-1-61219-534-6
ebook: 978-1-61219-535-3

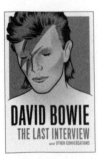

DAVID BOWIE: THE LAST INTERVIEW

"I have no time for glamour. It seems a ridiculous thing to strive for ... A clean pair of shoes should serve quite well."

$16.99 / $22.99 CAN
978-1-61219-575-9
ebook: 978-1-61219-576-6

MARTIN LUTHER KING, JR.: THE LAST INTERVIEW

"Injustice anywhere is a threat to justice everywhere."

$15.99 / $21.99 CAN
978-1-61219-616-9
ebook: 978-1-61219-617-6